The Keepers

Volume III

Hyacinths to Feed the Soul

Joan Rossiter Burney

Library of Congress
Catalog Card No. 96-96835

ISBN 1-57579-023-8

Illustrator: Mary Burney Sandberg

Printed in United States of America

 PINE HILL PRESS, INC.
Freeman, S. Dak. 57029

Dedication

This book is dedicated to you, my readers who are my friends, and my friends who are my readers. For the most part, the column's in this book, as in the first two books in this series, have been chosen by you as "Keepers." Throughout the years you have encouraged me with your letters, phone calls and visits. You have enabled me to keep on keeping on, enthusiastically! God bless you all!

Ode to Good Friends

It has been my joy
In life to find
At every turning of the road
The strong arm of a
Comrade kind
To help me onward
with my load.

And since I have
No gold to give,
And love alone must make amends,
My only prayer is
While I live,
God make me worthy
of my friends.
Amen!

(Author unknown)

Acknowledgements

A special thank you to my niece, Mary Burney Sandberg. No "Keepers" would be complete without the whimsical touch of this noted and award-winning artist.

A heartfelt thanks to my husband of **50** years, Kip, my family, and close friends, who have provided me with so much material.

Thank you, also, to the many people who have put up with me telling their stories in the columns herein. Each of you, wonderfully unique in your own way, are an important part of my life.

Last but NOT least, thanks to the talented folks at Pine Hill Press, Inc. Without their expertise, patient understanding and encouragement this book would never have been printed—and that's a fact.

God bless you all!

* * * * *

The essays in this book, except for two written especially for it, were chosen by our readers and appeared regularly as columns in the following magazines and papers: The Nebraska Farmer, The Colorado Rancher/Farmer, The Catholic Digest, The Omaha World Herald, The Norfolk Daily News, The Sioux City Journal, The Cedar County News, The Missouri Valley Observer, The Maverick Media Newspapers, The Catholic Voice and others. Many thanks to the editors and publishers of those fine publications.

Table of Contents

Chapter Four:
Parenting

Chapter Five:
Dealing with Difficulties

Chapter Six:
Dear Joanie

Chapter 7:
Growing Old Gracefully

Chapter Eight:
Encouraging Words

Preface
Hyacinths to Feed Thy Soul...

If of thy mortal goods thou art bereft
And from thy slender store two loaves alone are left,
Sell one, and with the dole,
Buy Hyacinths to feed the soul.

(Persian poet Eddin Saadi, 1184-1291)

When I am on my death bed trying to think of something wonderful to say to my greiving family and friends, something that will immortalize me in their minds and be passed down from generation to generation, I'm sure it won't be, "I'm sorry I didn't accumulate more 'things' to leave behind."

That why I love this tiny poem, written hundreds of years ago. It speaks to the fact that life is not about the pursuit of earthly goods, it's about the nourishing of souls.

I have a few earthly goods I'm fond of, you understand, and I have even enjoyed pursuing them.

But only to a point.

Because of events in my own life and the lives of people I love, I have learned that "things" are transient pleasure makers at best. At worst, they are trouble makers, because the pursuit of things begets the pursuit of things (as anyone who has bought increasingly larger R.V.s, homes, boats or cars will attest.) And in the final analysis, it's a waste of our limited "pursuit" time. True happiness has never been about accumulating material "things." It is about accumulating the blessings that replenish our soul.

My greatest hope, therefore, is that when I die, I will leave soul-replenishing memories, and a legacy of love, hugs, encouragement and faith, seasoned with great dollops of laughter. Hyacinths for the soul.

My columns, essays and personality profiles are all written to convey the message of the hyacinths, in one way or another. They share triumphs and tragedies, laughter and tears, and everything in between. They are written about family and friends and passing strangers. They tell about our abiding struggles, triumphs, and peculiar experiences, and reveal us as the unique and wonderful human beings we are when we quit trying to be who we aren't.

The columns in this book and the other two books in this series were, for the most part, chosen by readers who designated them "Keepers." In the letters accompanying the columns they shared stories of how a particular column uplifted, motivated, and/or amused them along the way. In doing so, they motivated and blessed me in ways for which I will be eternally grateful. That's why I am dedicating this book to them.

My fond hope and prayer is that at least one of the columns in this book, and maybe even two, will uplift, motivate or amuse you.

With that, I wish you God's blessings, dear reader, and a life strewn with Hyacinths.

Joan R. Burney

CHAPTER ONE

Inspirational People

In this chapter, dear readers, I give to you the unforgettable tales of the some of the wondrous characters who have enriched my life. I know, without a shadow of a doubt, that they will enrich yours too. Enjoy!

Hideaway Acres:
Conclave of Characters

Paris has it's Left Bank, traditionally the habitat of artists and poets and characters leading non-traditional lives. And we have our Hideaway Acres, a conclave of characters who live more or less cheerfully tumultuous lives on the Lewis and Clark Lake, near Crofton, NB., and Yankton, SD.

Not only did the adventurous Lewis and Clark pass this way on their historic journey, but Hideaway got it's name because Jesse James and his crew of notorious bandits are purported to have holed up on this very spot. It still has a wild and rustic air, in spite of the fine homes that nestle on the bluffs above the lake, because they are virtually hidden by the trees.

And, appropriately, the place has continued to harbor a multitude of characters.

Once in awhile we happen by to visit our friends, Shirley and Bob Bogue. It's always an occasion to remember. Sometimes an embarrassing one. It's embarrassing just to get the names straight of some of the characters living at Hideaway. You try to remember who's who when your introduced to Dutch and Bunny, Connie and Bonnie, and Dana and Barb.

The first embarrassing occasion happened years ago when we arrived at a party at Bogues and I was wearing a long dress. Everyone else was dressed in jeans. I didn't know Bogues as well then, and it was awful. Shirley saved me immediately by saying, "You must be going on to something dressy." Thankful for the out, I answered, "Well, as a matter of fact, we are."

Only thing was, then we had to leave the party early and the dressy place we went was home.

My embarrassment was lessened somewhat when I invited Shirley to a party at our house, and—erroneously thinking we were the dressy type—she arrived in a long dress. All of us were dressed in casual slacks.

Because of all this history between us, when she invited us to dinner a couple of weeks ago, I really appreciated it when she reminded me about the casualness of the dress at Hideaway. So, when Kip came home from the cattle sale and asked if this was a "suit and tie" party, I said, "No, it's very casual. Wear whatever you want." He was tickled. That's his kind of invitation.

You should have seen his face, not to say mine, when we arrived at Bogues house. You have never seen such a display of elegant attire. There we were in our ultra casual clothes, and Shirley and Bob, Connie and Bonny, Dutch and Bunny and Dana and Barb were dressed in what appeared to be sumptuous dinner attire. I'm talking gold lame' and velvet, flashy jewelry and the whole works.

And they were drinking from champagne glasses. At first glance it looked like a picture out of Harper's Bazaar.

We took in the scene in stunned silence. Kip gave me a look that would have slayed an elephant. And then the light dawned. We'd been had! At second glance, we could see that at least two of the velvet gowns were bathrobes.

To give you an idea of the low key camaraderie that is the status quo at Hideaway, as soon as we'd had our drink, the joke having been successfully perpetrated, Connie and Bonnie and Dutch and Bunny and Dana and Barb looked at their watches and said, "Well, Shirley says we have to go now."

Shirley had just invited them to play the joke on us, not to eat.

It's a state of affairs only the Hideaway clan could fully understand.

Eddie Hollis, 83 years old, Chauffeur
(Oct. 1995)

(And her 21 year old Opal.)

Usually, I don't take you along on my speaking excursions—unless something exciting happens. On my latest trip to Colorado, however, something happened. I got to meet Eddie Hollis and her car, and I was sure you'd want to meet them too.

My destiny was Limon. I was to do a workshop for the Colorado State Mothers, flying in and out of Denver the same day. It was my first flight to the new airport. It is beautiful. Restaurants and stores everywhere, and it is HUGE.

Eddie (pronounced EEDie) Hollis, my designated chauffeur, called to give me directions.

"You will come in on level five, which is B concourse. Walk to the escalators that take you to level three. Get on the train, go through concourse A to the terminal. Go back up to Level 5, then down again to the West Parking Area, door 404. I'll be there."

Say what??

Eddie had gone to the airport and traveled the route I'd have to take, just so I wouldn't get lost. It took me twenty minutes, walking as fast as I could walk, to get to door 404. There stood Eddie, a petite and pretty older woman with crisp short white hair, wearing a striking blue pants suit.

She greeted me enthusiastically and, walking briskly, led me to her shiny car. It looked brand new, but it was like no car I had ever seen.

I could hardly wait to question her, but she got to me first.

"I have a personal question to ask," said Eddie. "Could I borrow a little cash if I need it to get out of the airport?" (The Denver International Airport allows 70 minutes free time for people picking up or dropping off passengers.) "I put all the other things I needed in my car, but somehow I came off without my purse."

She explained, with the calm acceptance of one who knows a mole hill when she sees one, "We have no time to get my purse, so we will just have to make the best of it."

We did. We had a delightful visit. Eddie, I learned to my amazement, was 83 years old. Her car, a Buick Opal, was 21.

"They don't make them like this anymore," she said proudly. "It was made in Germany." It had, she said, developed a couple of little problems, but nothing she couldn't handle.

Eddie loves books and good stories, as do I. We shared and shared. She was all but sparkling as we talked, navigating the stick shift smoothly out of the labyrinth of DIA, and heading South down highway 70 to Limon. A good driver, but she doesn't "push" her car over 60 miles per hour. "It's not used to it," she said.

"My daughter scolded me for volunteering to do this. She thought the Mothers (group) could find somebody younger." My thought, too, although I was glad they hadn't.

"I don't feel that way," Eddie said, "As long as I feel good, I like to be of service.

(I learned later that they had asked other people, but Eddie was the only one not afraid.)

"Do your children worry about your driving?" I asked.

"I don't think so," she said, "but they do worry about this car. But you know, I've had it for 21 years...." As if that was a reason not to worry.

Eddie was the Colorado State Mother in the 1960s. She has been active since that time. Presently, she is putting out their newsletter (and picking up speakers.) She has been super active in Girl Scout work. She and her husband, a minister who died some 17 years ago, have a rustic cabin in the mountains, which was a get away for then and their four children. It was there that her scouts earned their wilderness badge.

"My children don't want me to drive in the mountains alone anymore," she said, "which is frustrating, but I still go. I just take someone with me."

As we headed back to Denver, she decided she'd check to see if she needed gas. To do so, she took a note book out of her glove compartment. It had neat little rows of mileage written on it. It turned out one of the "little problems" was a non working gas gauge. (They can no longer get parts.)

I had no business going to Colorado this weekend. Sometimes, however, I agree to things I have no business doing because I have an intuitive sense that I need to.

This time, I know why. I needed to meet Eddie. She may be 83, but with her enthusiasm for life and calm acceptance of adversities, she will be forever young.

What an inspiration!

My Sister June

I asked my sister, June, if I could write about her. She said, "If you just don't get too gushy." I'm not sure I can do that. I will try.

Several weeks ago my older sister, June Stockwell, had a stroke. It left her with some paralysis in her left side, a problem with balance, not much vision in one eye, no peripheral vision in either eye, and other problems. Her speech is fine, and she is sharp, but for June not to be able to take care of herself is not acceptable to her.

June has qualities I'd give anything to have. She is my mentor. An honors graduate of Duchesne in 1943 and an Aksarben Countess, she is extraordinarily self-sufficient, practical, and always in charge. She has had to be. She and her husband John, a regular in the Air Force, had eight boys and three girls, and they had them all over the world. She has had unimaginable challenges and mastered them. I'm not kidding. Try flying to Europe by yourself in the early fifties with three babies in diapers (cloth) and two on the bottle (glass!). Have two more babies while there, one premature, and an oldest son who develops polio. For starters!

She looks at problems unemotionally, and meets them head on. When I build something up all out of proportion, as I tend to do, she cuts to the core and puts it in perspective. When I start flying too high, she gently brings me down. Those familiar with the Briggs-Meyers personality test will understand. I am an ENFP, June, an ISTJ.

The Stockwells moved to Hartington when John retired, and when he died a few years back, June started accompanying me to my speeches and workshops. Some of you may have met her. A beautiful woman with short naturally curly gray hair, she is deeply religious and heavily into good health. So as a traveling companion, she greatly enhanced my knowledge of both, turning me on to anti-oxidants, and introducing the saints who are her special friends.

The irony of this stroke is that June was doing all she could do for her spiritual life and her health. The irony of all strokes is that they seem to happen to people who are intensely independent and private. People who most hate having other people take care of their intimate needs. We've had too many in our family, and I know getting past a sense of humiliation to acceptance is a giant step. Those of you who have walked this path as stroke survivors or care-takers could add volumes to this column.

June had her stroke in May in Gordon, Nebraska, where she was attending the graduation of her granddaughter, Hope, daughter of son Chris and Dr. Maggie Stockwell. Several of her children were there, so you can believe she got top notch care.

Chris brought her to Emmanuel in Omaha for rehabilitation. Just as I once was a smother mother, I found I'm a smother sister. The first day I sat through physical therapy with her, and other grueling tests, I could see she was exhausted. So we headed back to her room, and a nurse came up to tell us she was to have one more round of therapy. I protested vehemently. She was exhausted, I said, and she needed to get to bed. June held up her good arm to shut me up, and said sternly, "Of course I'll go to therapy, the sooner I learn to walk the sooner I get out of here." She was determined!

Out of there she got, and spent some time in the Hartington nursing home where we also have excellent therapists, and is now back in her three story house seeing if it will ever be possible for her to live there again. That's the good news.

The bad news is that this house is a giant obstacle course for her, with bedrooms on the second floor, walk-in shower on the third, and washing facilities in the basement. Her kids tried to insist on fixing a bedroom and shower downstairs and bringing the washer and dryer upstairs, but she won't let them. She is determined to get back to living as she was and driving again. However, specialists now indicate her eye sight might not improve, and driving might be out of the question. June, in her own style, is dealing with that reality— dragging with her, reluctantly, her children and her sisters.

All of us, most of Hartington, and all her many friends are praying for more recovery, and it could happen. We believe in miracles. And if we don't get our miracle, we take heart in the fact June is bright and cheerful, enjoys visiting, watching TV. and eating, so she has great potential for quality living. When the time comes, she will decide what path to take in her no nonsense way.

In some ways, however, it feels as if we're hovering on just this side of hell. You know what I mean?

So, if you have a moment free, and are so inclined, would you say a prayer for June and for her huge family who adore her?

And for her sisters.

Travels with Charlie: Fantastic!

Charlie and Jean Cook stopped by our little home away from home here in Arizona, having just come from a four wheel drive trip to view the desert-etched geoglyphs, 200 some figures, many more than 100 feet long, scratched in the dessert floor along the Colorado River from southern Nevada to the Gulf of California.

The strange scratchings in the desert, also called "rock-art sites" were largely undiscovered until this century. The first-known discovery was in 1932, when an airline pilot spotted a huge figure of a man just north of Blythe, California. Thought to have been carved by Native Americans over 5,000 years ago, the huge figures of men and serpents and lizards were, it is believed, messages to their gods and ancestors.

But this column is not about the geoglyphs, it is about Charlie Cook, who served as a pilot with Kip in World War II. An entrepreneur and adventurer, Charlie has added more than a little excitement to our lives over the years. Knowledge of the geoglyphs is one example. The figures, Charlie said, were "fantastic!" Who knew?

But then, for Charlie, everything is fantastic.

Typically, the Cooks were here just killing time, waiting for a call from the International Executive Service Corps to let them know when they could leave for Tienjin, China, and then Zimbabwe, where Charlie would be teaching executives there how business is done in the United States. They have already had two such adventures, one in Slovakia, which split from Czechoslovakia while they were there, and the other in Shanghai, China.

Both were, Charles has told us, "fantastic."

Charlie and Jean viewed the geoglyphs with Charlie's older brother Marshall and his wife Ruth of Sedona, Arizona, all former Nebraskans. They are part of a traveling group of retired executives and intellectuals who head out in their four wheel drives once a month to some exciting (and difficult to reach) destination which they have thoroughly researched. The more difficult to reach, the more interesting. Marshall, who worked on the White Horse Ranch as a young man, is also a rock hound and jewelry maker. He told me there are three precious stones in Nebraska. I'd never heard of them. Rock hounds would know, he said. But that's another column.

I think of the two Cook "boys," Charlie at six foot four and Marshall at six foot eight, as the gentle giants. Both say they are retired, but I think they don't quite understand the concept. Charlie charges through life with vigor, enthusiastically going from one adventure to another. Jean, his wife, a self described "small-town mid- western girl" follows in his considerable wake, telling him what to wear, where to turn and what road to take. You can bet, it is usually a road less traveled.

Their two daughters put a video together for their fiftieth anniversary. Pictures of Charlie and Jean with their family and world wide assortment of friends, of course. But also pictures of them schmoozing with dignitaries in all the countries they've visited while Charlie served as the executive director of Stanford Research International Institute, and then the Bechtal (sp?) corporation, where he solved problems for countries and corporations.

Charlie is also a licensed pilot, and a deep sea diver, and just recently, with fierce some determination, he has taken up golf. My advice? Stay out of his way!

A tour of the Cook home in Los Altos, California, is a tour of their lives. A tile given to them by the Shah of Iran graces one table, paintings from China and Japan hang on the walls. Fans sit about which were purchased while they were floating down the Yankstzi River. Irish afghans. Everywhere you look something else catches your eye, and everything has a story.

Following in Charlie's wake has put Jean in some interesting predicaments. My favorite, if not hers, was the time Charles, also a fisherman, caught the his first Marlin off of the coast Dominican Republic. Because he had to fly elsewhere, he sent Jean home carrying it's head, with what Jean called it's pointy "Pico." Jean had to meet Charles in Lincoln, where he was attending a tribute to Dr. Ted Jorguson, Charlie's mentor while earning a Ph.D.at U.N.L. "By the time I got to Lincoln," Jean said, " people were looking at me strangely. That fish head didn't smell at all good."

Charles has multiple degrees in physics, mathematics, engineering, and business administration, earned from such notable institutions as the U. of N. and Harvard. And he'll never quit learning. Or teaching. Jean, who has earned the equivalent of several doctorates just keeping up with Charlie, is also a born teacher.

We, two of their most avid pupils, have learned things we didn't even know we wanted to know. We've learned to appreciate China's culture, the mountains of the Dominican Republic, the economic conditions in

Slovak, and the desert-etched geoglyphs, and much more. Just thought I'd share a tad bit with all of you.

The Dendinger "Girls" Say Good Bye to the Old House

1996

The Dendinger girls dropped by this week. Although they haven't used the Dendinger name for many years, and some would say it's a stretch to call them girls, as Marian is 79 and Harriette, 77, they will always be"The Dendinger Girls" to my husband, Kip.

Dwight and Edna Burney, and the Burney "boys" Don, Wid, Dwight Jr., and Kip lived on a farm two miles up the road from Will and Martha Dendinger and their brood, Marian, Harriette, Nell and Kathleen and Roger. The two families were inseparable, even taking vacations together. Kip, the youngest Burney, just tagged along.

The Dendinger girls were here to celebrate the 60 anniversary of Marian's graduation from Mount Marty High School in Yankton, SD. (Six of the nine graduates were present.) They were having a "wonderful time." They seldom have any other kind.

Handsome, dignified women, who's looks belie their age, they come to our house and walk briskly to the picture window that looks over our farm. It's not our farm they see, of course, it's theirs. The Dendingers homesteaded this land. Their Dad was born the year the old house was built, 125 years ago. They climbed the big maple tree, fished in the creek, and played jokes on the "Burney Boys," short sheeting beds and putting dead mice under pillows, for starters

Will and Martha moved to California in later years, but the Burney/Dendinger bond remained strong. During World War II, Martha Dendinger pinned on Kip's wings when his Mom couldn't be there. Members of the extended Dendinger clan, hard working, talented, fun loving folks are still part of our lives. And I believe the benevolent ghosts of the Dendingers of yore watch over this valley.

No where near the ghost stage, the Dendinger girls live enthusiastically in the present. Harriette, who lives in Richmond, Ca. makes beautiful pottery, keeps her parish in freshly ironed linens, and says with some pride, "I'm the only old lady in my neighborhood who still mows my own lawn." Mirian manages her plethora of duplex's in her hometown of San

Jose,"by herself!" volunteers at the hospital and the airport and plays bridge with a vengeance.

Both"girls" take classes, ("We can never stop learning, you know") enjoy friends, manage investments and feel "very lucky" because they have their health and "can get to Mass every morning."

Harriette graduated from Creighton as a nurse in 1941, and went to work in August of that year at a local hospital at $35.00 a month. On December 7 of that year, everybody's life changed. On a tip from a nursing friend about higher wages, Harriett headed for California. By July 1, 1942, she was working as an industrial nurse in the Kaiser Ship Yard at the "unbelievable" salary of $135 a month.

She met her husband, Charles Stewart at the ship yards, and eventually took time off to have twin boys and a little girl. The Stewarts also started "buying up" vacant lots. Returning to nursing in 1957, she worked in emergency for 27 years, one of the few nurses, she says, who have worked part of four different decades.

The Stewarts sold their "vacant lots" (now holding seven houses and two duplexes) when Charley retired, and had time to enjoy a second home in Taho. Charley died six years ago, but Harriett still cherishes her weekends in Taho, as do her family and friends..

Marian led a less traditional life. After graduating in 1936, she went to business school, and then also headed for California. In 1942, with experience under her belt, she took a freighter through the Panama Canal intending to find work in New York. She got off the ship in Panama to call her sister, Kathleen, then working as a nurse on a banana plantation "400 miles back in the bush," and was invited to come run their office. "Why not?" Marian said to herself, and was on the next banana boat headed for the plantation. When she got there, she found she was expected to work in Spanish on a Spanish typewriter. Not to worry. "I picked it up quickly," she said.

After her time in the tropics, she headed for New York again, but this time she ended up in Guam. The year was 1948 and the government, intent on "rebuilding Guam," was hiring. Marian signed up for two years, and then two years more. "It was a "great experience." Two reasons. One was because Guam is only 36 miles long and four miles wide, so workers were given trips to exotic locations to keep them from becoming "island bound." The second, a "Scottish boy" named Bob Pyper, whom she married in 1951. Bob died in 1978, a year and a half after retirement from a Plumbing and Heating firm. "He missed work," Marian said."Some men shouldn't retire."

Chatting about growing up on the farm, the two distinguished ladies seemed to be girls again. "We made our own entertainment so, we had to be creative. We had nothing, but we were enriched rather than deprived."

The "girls" worry about the kids of today. "Too much TV. To little time to think their own thoughts."

Part Two
OLD HOUSE, RIP

The old house is gone. The open space in the trees where it once stood is now bare earth, like a newly covered grave. It was once vine covered and brimming with life, but—not lived in for many years—it had deteriorated to a point of no return.

I remember well the Spring of 1949, when Kip and I and Rob, not quite a year old, moved to the old house across the fields via a horse drawn wagon. We'd come home after going to college on the GI. bill, and lived briefly in Kip's folks home before moving to our newly purchased farm. We moved in March, which was traditional. Kip was eager to start farming. But the wretched winter left country roads bottomless, hence the trip across the fields. What an adventure!

Our farm was homesteaded by the Dendinger family. When the Dendinger girls, Marian Pyper and Harriett Stewart, visited in July, it was in terrible shape.

In their letter telling us they were coming, they'd written, "While we're there, we'd like a look at the old house." Oh no! Kip said "Ask them not to go in the house. It will make them sad."

They went in anyway. I would have done the same. And it did make them sad. They couldn't believe it was so small. It was, after all, the first "big house" built in this area. "Big meant two stories," Marian said. Their mother, Martha, built her own lily pool and lawn furniture, planted vines and flowers. It was a fine house. The biggest room was the kitchen, because "it was built for dancing." Dancing went on in every kitchen up and down this valley, with the Marshes and the Elliotts and the Millers and other valley families joining in.

When we moved in Kip built a counter through the middle of the kitchen. In our defense, we didn't know it was a dance floor. We lived there for seven years, until—with three little boys—we built the house we live in now, the"new" house. (Now forty years old.).

So the Dendinger girls memories are also ours, and although they live enthusiastically in today they cherish them, just as we do.

When they visited, I could visualize the house as it had been when they lived in it. I could hear the noise of kids climbing the old maple tree and playing ball. Then I realized it wasn't Dendinger kids I was seeing, it was Burneys— MY kids. I'd tapped into my own memories. The cheers and laughter I heard came from the motley array of Burneys and assorted relatives who always played ball when we gathered, right in the front yard. Ball fields were more important than grass in those days. Adults and kids of every size and shape gathered for the game. They teased each other good naturedly, and bickered about rules. (Often made up on the spot.) That was a big part of the fun.

It was the Dendinger girls calm acceptance of the necessity of the house's demise that gave us the courage to raze it.

After all, the old house had served gallantly, it had done its time. Keeping a sad old house around is no tribute to it.

The tribute lies in the vibrant memories of it as it once was, vine-covered and brimming with life, with a large maple tree for climbing, a front yard ball park, and a kitchen built for dancing.

Pearson's Passion for Plants Pays Off

When Craig Pearson was eight years old, he started growing plants. When ever his family visited friends, Craig "borrowed" clippings, rooted them, planted them, and according to his sister Cyndi, filled every nook of the Pearson home in Hartington.

His obsession grew. Summers with his Aunt Deahn Grove in Wayne, were spent one way, Pearson said, "we'd garden." At 13, he bought a plant for $3.00, nurtured it, and sold it for $25. However, Craig said, " I never thought of it as a business."

But a business it has become, and then some.

Called "Pearson and Company," it is located on East Main in Scottsdale, Arizona. A lush courtyard leads to a refurbished 1915 house, which is Pearson's gallery. It's the oldest free standing wooden structure in Scottsdale." Trees, plants, rugs, paintings, unique pots and other artifacts are tastefully displayed, and entice the discriminating buyer. It's an "ooh" and "ahh" experience.

A three dollar plant can still be purchased here, but most customers come for the services of the talented Pearson and his crew. Professionals in "Interior Plant Scape Design," they redecorate gardens and homes, finding just the right plant or artifact to suit a client's life style and taste. The costs range from modest to upwards of $150,000. Pearson's company designs for homes, estates, restaurants, hotels or business buildings. They provide the plants, plant or pot them, and then, if desired, they maintain them. What a deal! The success hasn't changed Pearson's first love, however, he's still happiest doing the "hands-on work," and dressed in grubbies.

Pearson's unique combination of talent and love of growing things is augmented by his passion for art and literature. He credits his love of literature to his high school English teacher Loxi Lober Wolfe, his passion for art to art teacher, Nona Modde Felber. (Attention teachers!) His confidence in his skills he attributes to the constant positive affirmation given to him by his parents, Neva and Dean Pearson. (Attention parents!)

Because he LOVES his work, and his clients love it too, by the time he's finished an "Interior Plant Scape Design" he has become part of their family.

This unique relationship was evident in a visit to the home of Jerry Apker, a "big time" art lover, the head Docent of Arizona State Art Museum, whose home nestles in the mountains overlooking Phoenix. Apker and Pearson greeted each other warmly, and immediately started clucking over special plants in her extensive formal and "wild flower" gardens. Her house, she said, was a "warehouse full of Mexican and Chicano art" and her gardens a "jungle" before Pearson took over. With stunning use of color, and a knack for knowing "just what should go where" Pearson changed all that into a magnificent artistic display. How magnificent? Well, it left me speechless. Me!

Apker says it makes her feel good just to look at it now, and adds, "He is a marvelous, marvelous talent—and so nice."

Nice he is. Thirty five years of age, low key and laid back, brown eyes shining with humor, he reminds one in stature and boyish good looks of Michael J. Fox. He doesn't take himself seriously. He describes buying trips in Indonesia, Egypt, Africa and Peru, like I'd talk about shopping at Dillards. He talks matter of factly about his work all over United States and in Europe for clients who "seem to like" what he did for them Arizona. He stays very busy, his cellular phone ringing constantly.

He saves his highest praise for his sister and partner, Cyndi, who, he says, has "all the business sense," and serves as his left brain. A tour of his new home ("Cyndi said I could buy it!")is a tour of his life. It is decorated eclectically with collections or art and artifacts from all over the world, interspersed with "funky" fifties furniture rescued from his "Grandma Dempster's" basement in Orchard.

How does a young man get from borrowing clippings to becoming a jet-setting Interior Land Scape Designer? He says, with a grin, "I've been really fortunate."

Fortunate, yes. But hard work and a hunger to always learn more and do better, has more to do with it. When life opens a door for him, he has always been ready to go through— and redesign what's on the other side.

It all started when Pearson graduated from Hartington High School in 1978. He loaded his dad's camper with 150 plants, and headed for Arizona to work in a nursery.

Carol and Lee Ackerman, who owned an estate on Camelback Mountains, served as mentors for both Cyndi and Craig. Cyndi followed Craig out to Arizona to finish high school, started her own house cleaning business, where the Ackerman's found her, hired her as a Nanny and then as manager of their personal finances. Also impressed with Craig's talent, the Ackermans helped him start his own business and he was on his way!

Can you believe that?" Craig asks. It's not hard.

Humbly aware of his good fortune, Pearson "tries to give something back," volunteering for work for Desert Botanical Garden, abused children and Aids Victims.

This is but a brief synopsis of the on-going story of the Pearson "kids," who grew up under my nose in Hartington. I share it because it is a powerful illustration of the influence of positive parents and good teachers.

Their numbers are many, and they KNOW who they are. To them I say, Congratulations! God bless you all.

Ferdie and Joe,
Legends in Their Own Time

I've been giving much thought, lately, to two folks who are no longer with us. One was part of my life, and one I wish had been.

The one I wish I'd known better was a marvelous, generous, talented, funny man, the late Joe Radosti. A much beloved banker from Creighton, Nebraska, the stories about Joe are legendary. Stories of how he stuck by his beleaguered farm customers during the crisis, of his generosity to his community and his friends, and of his famous tomato recipe. Lately, they've been of how much he was loved in Creighton, and how much he is missed.

He came into our lives by way of his classic bright yellow golf cart. We played in the Creighton Couples Open, and Betty Radosti, Joe's wife, kindly loaned our hosts, Eldon and Jo Hartman, Joe's golf cart for us to use. Fully equipped, complete with stereo, refrigerator, and the works, it looks like a Rolls Royce. We have used a "loaner" from the company fixing our burned out cart, and we're grateful for it. But it has no top, and lurches. Having experienced Joe's golf cart, we'll never be the same. We even golfed better than we know how.

Joe's tomatoes were served again, in his honor, at the Plainview Golf Course's annual sweet corn feed. Golfers from miles attend, our guys included. Joe and his buddies always drove to Omaha to get just the right olive oil for his famous recipe. The olive oil wasn't expensive, Joe always said, but the trip got a little expensive.

Passing golfers, seeing Joe's golf cart, gathered around us expectantly. Seemed that Joe always kept a refrigerator full of beer to share with his golfing buddies. If only we'd known.

The other person I've been thinking about is auctioneer/ philosopher (aren't they all!) Ferdie Peitz. He was my mentor, my personal historian, subject of a multitude of my columns, and my friend. He was recently inducted into Nebraska's Rock and Roll Hall of Fame, along with the Skylon Ballroom he built in 1961. I dragged Kip, and our friends, Shirley and Gerald Stevens, to the ceremony. It was, of course, a Rock Concert. We are folks who love (and are) Golden Oldies. But we stuck around as long as our ears could stand it. It was fun.

The Hall of Fame and the Nebraska "Rocks" Concert, was founded in 1994 by Jim Casey, a '64 graduate of Norfolk Catholic. His "Smoke Rings," and the other bands put on an impressive show.

Ferdie hosted the Guy Lombardo, Shep Fields, Woody Herman and Lawrence Welk bands, along with all the burgeoning young rock and roll bands. So, he must be pleased with what's happening to his ball room, now operated by our young Hartington entrepreneur, Jim Topf. Jim has renovated the historic dance hall, and is breathing new life into it with a variety of dances and shows. With his upbeat outlook, sense of humor, and pleasant personality, he could become another Ferdie Peitz. That's the highest complement I can give

Ferdie's always spouted axioms, and one guides my life. It is: "There's good in everybody. It just takes a little time to find it in some."

Honoring loved ones, whether with a tomato tradition, or a plaque, or telling warm stories, keeps them with us in spirit, so they can continue to enliven our lives. Instead of bemoaning their deaths, we celebrate our great fortune in being part of their lives in their too brief time on this sad old earth.

Lori Potter,
Communicator of Achievement

When I read the note from Lori Potter handed to me by the desk clerk at the Marriot Hotel in Charlotte, NC., I cried.

Kip and I were in Charlotte for convention #59 of the National Federation of Press Women. Peggy Pond, the President of the North Carolina Press Club, had issued us a special invitation, which included a few days at a lake in South Carolina after the convention.. We've become fast friends of the Ponds, having bonded on a pre-tour "Bus Ride from Hell" years ago. Kip was to hang out with Bob. I planned to enjoy Press women and men, friends from Iowa and South Dakota included, and stretch my mind at workshops.

The most important reason we were there, however, was to support Nebraska Press Women's Communicator of Achievement, Lori Potter, regional editor of the Kearney Hub. Lori is a wonder. Anything she does, she does well. She led the feisty if brilliant members of NPW with wisdom and confidence, through perilous times, gaining undying appreciation, respect and love.

For me, the business part of the meeting would be a no brainer, because Lori was there. She would represent our President, Judy Nelson, take notes to present at our next meeting, take the needed pictures, give Nebraska's report and, in her no nonsense manner, vote our local affiliate's often controversial views.

This convention was to be HER convention. She was pumped for it. She'd won national prizes, and was up for the CoA. awards.

My job? To get her a corsage. That I could handle.

But the note at the desk changed all that. She wrote, "We just got in from a wonderful pre-tour of the Asheville area. I had a message from home that my dad died this morning. This was not a big surprise as he's been failing greatly...I hesitated to come at all, but he had been no worse for the past weeks. And Mom said I should come, because he could have stayed the same for a long time."

Lori's family is as close as a family can be. Her Dad and Mom are great people, and have always supported their children 100%. To lose her Dad, even if it was expected, would be a terrible heart break. I hurt for her. When I called Judy Nelson, I couldn't even read Lori's letter to her coherently.

Lori, bless her heart, left me with specific marching orders so I could carry out her missions. She told me how the board decided to vote on amendments, assuring me "if any amendments are made from the floor, I know NPW members will support any decision you make." Yeah, right.

I knew also that I needed to bring home to Lori everything that was passed out and a few things that weren't. She's a saver.

But the paragraph that got to me was this one:

"I sure hate missing the CoA banquet. I'm so proud to have been selected to represent my friends and idols in NPW. I know this won't happen, but if for some incredible reason my name is called, would you please say a few words for me about how special my NPA and NFPW friends are to me."

That was the paragraph I read to the gathered throng when Lori's name was called as the First Runner Up. Everyone missed having Lori there. There wasn't a dry eye in the house.

For Lori, as young as she is, it's a fantastic recognition and a well deserved one.

The Roses: Been There, Done That

Dr. Bill and Marie Rose should have a bumper sticker on their car reading "Been There, Done That."

They've traveled to every state in the Union, and almost every continent, and two years ago, at 82 and 78 respectively, they took a balloon ride, a gift from their three daughters. "It was the only mode of transportation we hadn't tried," they said, "It was wonderful!"

Eyes sparkling with humor, cute as the proverbial bug's ear, Dr. Bill and Marie live in Sunland Village, Mesa, Arizona, a few doors down from where we lived for three enjoyable months. Now 84 and 80, lively as crickets, they are an inspiration.

The Rose family lived in Leadville, Colorado, across the street from Molly Brown. (The Unsinkable). Following in the footsteps of his dentist father and grandfather, Rose served this "colorful" town until he retired in 1967 at 55, to spend more time with his "helpmate of 30 years." A Leadville paper said Dr. Rose was responding to "the inherent individualism of his pioneering ancestors."

Leaving Leadville was difficult, Dr. Rose said, but "I learned when I was very young that nobody is irreplaceable." Chuckling, he told the story of how he worked in a "movie house" for $4.50 a week from age 12 years to 18. "I knew the place would fall down without me. In fact, I was positive of it. But, you know, I left and it survived—for over fifty more years. That lesson has stuck with me."

Stories abound in the Rose home, as do historical artifacts, art, china and crystal. A talented artist, from a family of talented artists, Dr. Rose has had several hobbies (read that "obsessions) since retirement, changing from one to the other when, he said, "I ran out of people to give things to."

An accomplished wood-worker, Dr. Rose's first phase was building things—such as their retirement home on the Frying Pan River in Colorado. The intricately designed coffee table in the Rose living room today gives eloquent testimony to phase one.

His second phase was making gold and silver jewelry. Marie's collection of silver and turquoise pendants, bracelets and rings made this jewelry lover's mouth water. Marie says, "I never wear one that people don't want to know where to buy it."

After this came his "glass" phase. Intricately cut , brightly colored stained glass panels grace the front door and decorate lamp shades. Some lovely pieces reside in a closet, because "I told you, I ran out of people to give them too."

Dr. Rose's latest interest is working on his computer. It will last awhile, as he's writing the history of his family and Leadville. Our mutual interest in Macintoshes brought us together. And—yes—he is also a good writer. Some people can do it all!!

Marie also keeps "more than involved" as a life member of three groups she considers well worth her time, P.E.O., Questers and the Woman's club.

Like many of their peers, after retirement the Roses traveled in increasingly sophisticated R.V.s, and arrived in Arizona as snow birds, staying a few weeks. They loved it, and for 17 years made their winter home at the Fiesta R.V. Park where Marie starred in the Kitchen Band and danced the Cha Cha for special occasions.

Arizona increasingly felt like home, and keeping two homes going became a burden, so eight years ago the Roses bought their present home. After all, Doc said, "We've out lived most of our friends in Colorado."

The Roses exemplify the second reason people like it in Arizona, perhaps more important than the weather. And that is that they and all the people around them have a "young at heart" attitude, which, it would seem, keeps them that way.

When we arrived in Arizona, we were told we'd recognize winter Arizonans because they'd be healthy and tanned and the first thing they'd ask is, "have you seen my ball?" They not only golf, they walk, they clog, they line-dance, they square dance, they sing, they act, they play cards. These people are active. They are BUSY.

Although it's easier to be active when it's warm, the secret is not the weather. Not everybody can go South, nor do they want to. It's attitude.

It's enthusiasm for life. And that happens wherever we choose to have it happen.

Unlike the Roses, who are having trouble planning their next trip because "we've been everywhere we want to go," most of us have places we want to go and things we want to do. So, we better get with it.

Even though, occasionally, we might look longingly at our recliners, considering what a joy it might be just to lean back, whine, and listen to our arteries harden.

Marge "Let The Good Times Roll" Dietz

Marge Dietz is a character, a practical joker bar none, with such an infectious laugh just to hear her is to have a good time. She loves to tell stories on herself, such as the time she started her wash in the basement of her home and decided to throw in the clothes she had on. Walking up the steps stark naked, she met the man delivering the groceries. She thought it was funny. Hysterical even. The delivery man? Well, no where is it recorded what he thought. Marge said, "He never looked me in the eye again." No wonder!

The Dietz's were one of the founding couples of our Sunday Night Bridge Club, which has been meeting for nearly fifty years. (We were all ten when it started.)

Marge called me last December and said, "Are you ever coming to Omaha?" I said I was flying in for some speeches. She INSISTED she'd pick me up, I'd stay with her, and she'd take me to my speech. "We'll get some quality time together," she said.

And we did! We had so much catching up to do, that we kept talking after we went to bed in our separate bedrooms. And laugh! I felt like a kid at a slumber party.

The best part was to come, however. On the drive to Kearney we saw thousands of Sandhill cranes. This was a first for Marge. Seeing the Sandhill's Cranes is a thrill. Seeing them with a good friend is better yet.

Do you ever ponder why it is that we get so involved with the "busyness" of living, the "quantity" of life, as it were, that we don't take time to be with good friends, the quality of life.

Marge is one of those friends. Wife of the late Dr. Roger Dietz, an optometrist, she lived in Hartington and enlivened our lives for many years. They moved to Bellevue some years ago. They have a son Greg and a daughter Kerry, who follows in her father's foot steps.

Marge is a kick. To see her is to love her. Her humor is outrageous, her attitude refreshing, and time with her is well spent. To give you a taste, here's a poem she had on her refrigerator. It might tickle you. It did me.

(Remember, It's a joke.)

When I'm an Old Lady—

Then I'll live with my children and bring them great joy—
To repay all I've had from each girl and boy
I shall draw on the wall and scuff up the floor;
run in and out without closing the door.
I'll hide frogs in the pantry, socks under my bed,
Whenever they scold me, I'll just hang my head.
I'll pester my children when they're on the phone,
As long as they're busy, won't leave them alone.
Hide candy in closets, rocks in a drawer,
and never pick up my clothes from the floor.
I'll stuff up the plumbing and deluge the floor.,
As soon as they've mopped it, I'll flood it some more.
When they correct me, I'll lie down and cry.
Kicking and screaming, not a tear in my eye.
I'll take all the pencils and flashlights, and then,
when they buy new ones, I'll take them again.
I'll spill glasses of milk to complete every meal,
eat my banana and just drop the peel.
Put toys on the table, spill jam on the floor,
I'll break lots of dishes as though I were four;
What fun I shall have, what joy it will be—
To live with my children like they lived with me.

Tale of Two Stuckenhoff's, Builders Extroardinaire

In the 1958 Hartington Jubilee book there is an in depth interview of Henry Stuckenhoff, who was then 96 years old. Mr. Stuckenhoff came from Germany at the age of 21 with considerable skill in the building trade. He settled in St. Helena, later moving to Hartington, and then, often, where-ever his work took him. He built homes, bridges, barns and imposing edifices still in use today, such as picturesque churches in Bow

Valley, Fordyce and Wynot, and the Library and Court House in Hartington.

He not only watched the towns in this area grow up out of the prairie, he helped build them "brick by brick, board by board and building by building."

His son, Dr. H. E. Stuckenhoff, didn't go into the building profession because, he said, "My father said, 'don't get involved in this kind of work.'" In spite of that, "I tried it for one summer," he said, "and that was it!"

But he is following in his father's footsteps, building foundations, albeit financial ones, that support the educational institutions and students of his Alma Maters. His "building of foundations" will also last, as his father's has, long after he is gone.

His generous gifts of one millions dollars to Creighton University and to the Holy Trinity and Cedar Catholic School foundations in Hartington, boggle the mind of those of us who part with a lot less money and do it reluctantly. He likes these kinds of gifts, he indicated, because the principle can never be touched, only the interest can be used. "That's important," he said.

My friends, Gerry and Shirley Stevens, and I had the privilege of visiting with Dr. Stuckenhoff in his home in Litchfield Park, Arizona. And, although mighty fragile at 94 years, he still has a twinkle in his eye and his inherent sense of humor was evident as he shared stories he obviously relished. .

In fact, he liked to tell them so much that when his wife of thirty years, Marge, came home, and we interrupted our conversation to visit with her, he let us visit for a few minutes, and then said, "But I haven't finished my story."

I told him I felt we were talking to a true hero. He chuckled at that, saying modestly and sincerely, "I'm not the hero, that was my father."

Dr. Stuckenhoff's mother died in 1903 when he was three months old. From that time on, he said, his father "danced him" between the Sister's convent in Hartington and Mrs. Don Felber. He remembers both experiences fondly.

He earned three degrees, first a Bachelor of Science, then a degree in pharmacy, and, finally, after working at his brother-in-law Alex Schulte's drug store in Wynot (later to move to Hartington) for five summers, he earned his M.D.

The story we interrupted was about going to a dance after he got his M.D. A fellow shook hands with him and said, "What are you going take now, Doc, Law?" "He seemed to think I was an educated ass." Doc said, 70 some years later.

After getting his M.D., Dr. Stuckenhoff moved to Casper, Wyoming, where he practiced medicine till he retired. He donated the money to the

Catholic Schools because, he said, "I've been very fortunate, and I wanted to give something back." It's his firm belief that "Catholic schools are excellent models of education."

Dr. Stuckenhoff grew up like most young man of his era, ice skating on the dam behind the Sisters' Convent south of Hartington, hunting musk rat on Bow Creek, playing first base on the Wynot ball team, and attending "the biggest and best event of the year," the "Scheutzenfest" at Bow Valley. (Which has been reinvigorated.)

He loved to dance, remembering fondly dancing at the Legion Club at Hartington. "I was a regular twinkle toes then!" he said, eyes twinkling.

Marge says—maybe then—but not any more. She told of their dancing on a cruise they took last year through the Panama Canal. "We stood up," Marge said, "and Doc just stood there. He didn't move. So I started moving. Somebody had to. He said, 'you're leading!' That was the end of that!" Doc just grinned.

Dr. Stuckenhoff has spent much time in Hartington, visiting his sister Anna Schulte and her family. What has impressed him, he said, is "how Hartington has survived." Not every town could withstand the bouts of adversity as Hartington has, Doc said, nor could all people. His example was his old friend, Jack Spork, who sold his drug store and left town because, Spork said, "I'm not going to live around here any more and pray for rain."

Dr. Stuckenhoff has added not only money to the bricks and boards and buildings his father built, he has added something less tangible but more important and that is his faith in the institutions he is supporting. What a boost to morale that kind of faith is.

The accomplishments of the students whose lives he has touched, and of the people whose lives they touch, will be his monument . That will go on forever.

(Think about that, ALL you generous givers to good causes, and rejoice!!)

"Birds" of a Feather
Honoring Home Town Heroes

In every community, no matter how big or how small, there are special folks who move in, stay for awhile, and then move on, but leave an indelible mark. Most often, we don't get the opportunity to say thank you. Last week we did.

Such a man is Rubin Bird, a resident of Hartington from 1932 to 1957. He and his wife Trudy, his son Robert and his grandson Justin, came into town to accept a Lifetime Achievement Award from the Alumni Association of Cedar Catholic. A spry 82, eyes glinting with humor, Rubin said he was "flattered beyond belief."

The award is well deserved. In a short speech, notable for it's humility and sincerity, he told of his coming to Hartington. "My close buddy and life-long friend, Sy Hurowitz, suggested we form a partnership with his uncle, Ben Narinsky, and run a General Merchandise store. We called it the People's Store. The depression was really severe at that time, and opportunities were non-existent. The partnership was a great opportunity for me, and in hindsight, I could not have made a better decision."

In two years time his partners went their own way, and Rubin became the sole owner of the People's store. His goal, he said, was to beat local competition, build his own business and bring more business into Hartington. He did it. He was a master at the use of loss leader items, long before other grocery stores understood their value, generous in granting credit, and a promotional genius. (Genius is my word, not his.) One of his promotions was to give every baby born in Cedar County their first pair of baby shoes. We have big families in Cedar County, so that was no small thing.

Rubin Bird came to town in the "dirty thirties," when times were truly tough. "Granting credit" required faith and guts. Rubin did just that. To this day people say "Our folks would never have made it through the depression years if Rubin Bird hadn't given them credit."

He was more than just a purveyor of credit. He was an ambassador of good will, a community leader, an innovator and an entrepreneur. All of that.

He loved young folks, and spoke fondly of the local students who worked for him. "They were terrific help to me," he said, "and I know having those jobs made a big difference to them." He supported sports, took young people to games, helped them through troubled times, and got involved in a project with County Agent Jim Ross to raise litters of pigs for 4-H kids. Rubin said, chuckling, it turned out to be an "Interesting, expensive, but worthwhile project."

Rubin remembered the Golden Spike Days celebration n Omaha, with a grin and more than a hint of mischief in his eyes. He and my brothers, Lawrence and Vincent Rossiter, organized a caravan of railroad cars that "picked up party go-ers between Hartington and Omaha." Legendary stories came out of that trip, but Rubin would only say, "What a party that was!"

Another memory included coming to the rescue of Margaret and Gerald Lammers on the day of their wedding. They were snow-bound and couldn't get to the church. They called him to come get them with his store truck. He did better than that, he sent horses and a slay. "It was much more romantic!" he says now.

This is just a taste of Rubin Bird, who's still active in his Budget Car Rental business Los Angeles. As you read it, I'm sure the "Rubin Birds" of your community will come to life.

In closing his little talk, Rubin said, "Hartington will always be in my heart."

That's only fair. Because Rubin, Trudy and their family will always be in ours.

Wintering in Arizona!

We've spending a few months in Arizona every winter now. The warm weather is good for Kip. He girds himself every day with his anti-arthritic pills and heads to the golf course. He's not happy with his game, even with a hole-in-one, but he enjoys his golfing buddies, Eldon, John and Bert, and we're just happy he's playing at all.

Our home away from home is a lovely three bedroom southwest style home on the third hole of the golf course in Sunland Village, a retirement community in Mesa. We rented it for three months in '96, and liked the place and our neighbors so much that we bought it in '97, completely furnished. The ghosts of the former owners, the much loved Falkenberg's, hover. Most especially they are apparent in all the music equipment here, the most astonishing being an organ in the corner of the living room. Music lover that I am, you know I'm a happy camper!

The majority of people here, vibrant and youthful looking folks, own their homes. Many of them live here year around. Those who don't , like our friends Eldon and Jo Hartman of Creighton, live here several months. Therefore, they are NOT snow birds, they inform us, they are winter Arizonans.

Eldon and Jo are the reason we found Sunland Village. Eldon was an I.B.P. buyer who bought Kip's cattle every week. He had lunch with Kip every Monday for some 29 years. Eldon, and his wife, Jo, became fast friends.

Everybody here is friendly. Among the nicest people in the world are our next door neighbors, Betty and Ray Kummer. They are retired farmers from North Dakota, and wonderful characters. Ray has one arm gone (farm accident) but plays golf very well, thank you very much, with his prosthesis. He's an avid farmer and carpenter, and when he isn't farming at his place, he's planting cacti at ours. Our very first day in our house, Betty came to our back door with a coupon so that we could buy a half gallon of milk for 99¢. Not THERE'S a neighbor.

The Kummers and we are at opposite ends of the pole, politically, but we have more important things in common, such as a love for bridge. We've played a little bridge, too. Mostly, we meet on our drive ways or patios, introducing each other to our mutual passing parade of guests. But we've established a fond relationship. Yesterday, I came out in a color- coordinated outfit, unusual for me, and Betty called over, "You look pretty good for a Republican!"

The golf course is a 31 par executive course, which is—to me—a delight. My game is straight and down the middle, and it's made for me. It is great fun to pity the poor folks who hit long (and uncontrollable) balls. Son Bill has blessed a few roof tops and back yards with his.

The house is lovely, but my favorite spot is the patio. That's where we gather with our friends and sit in absolute tranquility every evening, in the midst of this huge city, watching the brilliant Arizona sunsets.

Although I miss the people at home, and even—believe this or not— miss the snow (not the ice!!) this part of our trip on the on-going journey of life is going to be okay. You all drop by and see us!

Honey

Honey Woolsey, a look of frustration on her usually sunny conti-nence, said "Well, think of it this way, Joanie, it isn't too smart to golf good when you're establishing your handicap, anyway."

A positive person, always looking at the bright side, she'd reached the bottom of the barrel. It was the last (and least) encouraging thing she could think of to say.

Until then she'd said such things as, "At least it's straight." Or "you're not in any trouble, anyway." Or "Don't worry, It will come."

However, it wasn't always straight, I *was* in trouble, and it (my latent golfing ability) never came.

I said to Honey as we tootled unhappily along the fairways in our golf cart, "Having two positive thinkers try to be positive about something negative gets almost sickening, doesn't it?"

She laughed heartily.

Honey always laughs heartily. Her laughter ripples over the hills and ponds of the "pasture" that is in our winter back yard, a comforting sound to all who know and love her. Their heads go up much as ours do at the honking of the return of the Sandhill's Cranes, and they smile. Honey's here. All's right with the world.

The Woolsey's moved away for awhile, but moved back because Honey missed her friends here. She has a multitude, because she is an optimist who has refreshingly realistic outlook on life's inevitable diffi- culties. "That's the way it is." she says. "Live with it."

Fortunately for me, if unfortunately for her, our paths crossed last November on this very Sunland Village Golf Course. A remarkably young 76-year-old, Sunny has been many times champion of the Women's league. Tired of competition, however, she's decided to "float." A "floater" is a person who plays when the spirit moves her with whomever is available to play with. As a renter, which we were then, I could only golf in the Women's League as a guest. Sunny, in her ultimate kindness asked me be her guest. The kindly pros in the club house said "guest of a floater" was the lowest designation a golfer could have.

Being the lowest designated golfer didn't phase me. I came to golf late in life at the insistence of my husband, a born-again golfer. Golf has been simply a game to me, and a silly one at that. Who could possibly get serious about chasing a tiny golf ball around a manicured pasture? As someone once said, "golf just ruins a good walk."

Things happen in one's life, however, and adjustments have to be made. When spending time in Arizona became necessary because of Kip's health, and this manicured pasture turned up in our back yard, I realized golf was going to be part of my life for eleven months out of the year. There are those who'd be ecstatic at that turn of events. I am not one.

Good sport that I claim to be, however, I decided to look at golf in a different light. Floating with Honey would be a good start, although she gives hints reluctantly, and only when pushed.

Also, I took a lesson—and practiced with a broom.

I swear I improved.

Which brings me to another dramatic adjustment in our lives. Home for Christmas, snuggled in our little red farm house with a blizzard raging, we got a call from Chuck Falkenberg, from whom we rented the house we live in Arizona. He wanted to sell immediately.

Kip, who had never had much intention of buying a second home, felt the ache in his bones that had returned in the frigid weather, looked out of the window the blowing snow, considered the reasonable price, and said, "Okay."

Under the hovering, protective eyes of our Realty-knowledgeable sons, Chuck and Bill, it was soon a done deal.

Upon our return after Christmas, therefore, the first thing Kip did was join the golf club, signing me up for the Lady's League. So the first time I played with Honey in 1991, a floater now, myself, I was establishing my league handicap. It all had to be very business-like, very un-Joanie. I must have been nervous.

Nonetheless, I could hardly wait to play with Honey to show her how I'd improved. I visualized the amazed look on her face, and heard the golf course ring with her joyous cheers.

Well, forget that. The "lesson," with the broom deserted me. Honey's hints left my mind. It was a debacle.

Someday the fact that I was establishing my handicap may comfort me. As well the last positive thing Honey said to me when we finished. "You'll be in good shape to win the award for 'most improved.'"

But I doubt it.

I share this sad tale with you because I think many of you will relate. Although, somehow, I doubt anybody at home will have an ounce of sympathy for anyone playing golf in Arizona.

Father Rick Arkfeld Goes Home

Life's hard.
God's good.
Let's Dance.

One of Father Rick Arkfeld's greatest gift's was his sense of humor. The message above, printed on his favorite T Shirt last time I spoke to him, spoke eloquently of this gentle priest.

In February of 1986, Father Rick Arkfeld learned he had cancer, and only a few months to live. "I don't know that I was prepared for it," he said, "but I was excited because it was a new way of teaching and preaching." In a homily to his parishioners, he asked them "not to pray for a miracle, or that I would be healed. If God wants to heal me, then I'll live as long as God wants me to live. I asked them to pray that I give a good example."

Whatever happens, he said joyfully, "I am a son of God and I am going to the Kingdom and I am terribly, terribly excited."

God did indeed have different plans. The cancer went into remission, and Father Rick's excited entry into the Kingdom had to be put on hold. Looking through his "window called death" and realizing that his respite was doubtless temporary, he decided from that moment on his ministry would be to bring healing to the grieving.

"The right words always came to me," he said, a gift that overwhelmed him, and one for which he never took any personal credit. "It's never been me," he said, "It's always been the Lord."

He came to trust his gift, and if people in turmoil showed up around Father Rick, they got help, whether they wanted it or not. "God blessed me with the gift to recognize people who are struggling, and gave me the courage to go up to them and say, 'You need help—if you can't tell me what's troubling you, tell some one, or it will destroy you.'"

People were hungry for his message of God's love, and he carried it to them with retreats, speeches, appearances on radio and TV, even with sometimes precarious health. It would be impossible to estimate the number of lives he's touched.

A few years back, musing over the fact he was still alive, he said, "You know, I'm a little embarrassed about not dying. But then, someone comes who needs my help, and I know why I'm still here.

As sick as he has been this year, his humor still came through. He was an unremorseful tease. "I love to harass people," he said. And he loved it when they harassed him back.

He reached across every age level with his humor, from the little children in his beloved Ponca, whom he called "my hairy little varmints" to the elderly in the day care center near his home. Humor is a part of his healing gift. especially for old friends in recent months as it seemed his death was "finally" eminent. It kept them from drowning in their own tears. His gift of joyous laughter was life affirming, touching both on the here and the hereafter.

It took awhile, in the beginning, for his close knit family to be comfortable with his ability to laugh in the face of death, but he said, "I knew I'd been successful when one of my brothers called to ask what the Doctor told me at one of my check ups. I told him that the Doctor said the cancer could turn up anywhere, even in my brain. My brother said, 'don't worry about that Rick, it would die of starvation'."

Typical of his self-deprecating humor, was his story about getting a call from a woman who'd heard his tapes and desperately wanted him to give a workshop for the people with whom she worked in her Hospice. He sent a tape, which was reviewed by the two nuns in charge. They sent it back. Father Rick, laughing uproariously, said, "They wrote, 'we're not interested in entertaining the dying, we're interested in preparing them for death.' "

"I'm a lucky man," Father Rick said. "I got the warning to get ready, and then I had this wonderful opportunity to teach others to die gracefully." From the first, he said, he never cried about his cancer, or was sad, or angry or anxious. In fact, he said, chuckling, "I loved talking about it. When I went into remission people would ask me how I was, and I'd still say, 'I'm in constant pain, have sleepless nights, and can hardly eat a bite.' They'd say, 'but I thought the cancer was in remission?' And I'd say, 'It is. But I still love talking about it."

"I've cried when I heard a song that moves me, because I think if it can be this beautiful here, what must it be like in heaven?" he said, "and I have cried for the sadness of those who think I'm leaving them. But just to cry for myself—I haven't done that. I don't understand exactly why, but I think grace comes when you need it."

These last months, however, he admitted he was sad. Typically, however, it wasn't for himself, It was, he said, "Because I'm not going to be here for the people I love when they need me."

His faith remained rock solid, however, and his dedication to the church caused him to shake his head about "Catholics who run away from the Lord and just want to do their own thing. Who chase after money, or sports, or whatever they can, in order to escape their problems and their families."

"I pray that those people will come to know what it is they are looking for, and that is the love of God in their lives."

"People who move away from God need to understand that He never moves. He's always there waiting."

Father Rick has reason to know this. He was ordained in 1962, and at that time and he said, "It was strange. I stood outside of myself looking on, so happy that an Arkfeld was becoming a priest."

In June, 1974, in an agony of conscious, he quit the priesthood. "Everything was hard," he said, "and I was frightened of preaching." Four an a half years later, he was asked to preach at the funeral of the daughter of a good friend. "I wanted to do this," Father Rick said. It was only after he'd agreed that he remembered what an agony it was for him to preach. "I could not prepare one word." But a "strange and wonderful" thing happened, the Holy Spirit took over. "And I listened to myself preach a sermon I never heard before...it was amazing."

"I finally got the message: if I got out of the way, the Holy Spirit would take over." Father Rick would like to tell the newly ordained priests to quit worrying, quit pushing themselves. "We must let the Holy Spirit take over."

From that time one, he said, "I never prepared another sermon, and I never wanted to get out of the pulpit again. I just spoke from my soul. "

Ironically, Father Rick said, it was the two things he was most frightened of, speaking and cancer, that took over his life. "The Lord just zapped me with them, and said get with it."

He'd like people to remember that perfection is not a human attribute, even for priests, that every one falters and has dark nights of the soul. "Sometimes the devil tempts us, even in our strengths, and fills us with doubt."

"We can't pretend he isn't around," he said, "for he is. But the truth is, the devil has no power over us unless we give it to him. Remember, he lost! So he isn't anybody to run away from in fear. Sometimes, however, *God uses sin to bring us home to him.* Sin makes us realize we're human, and brings us to a point when we just have to admit we need God's help, we can't do it by ourselves.."

There was a time, he said, when "I was in despair, and couldn't shake it. Every day I would go to the church and pray for God's help. Over and over I'd pray 'you know I love you God.' But the despair remained. Then, one day, when I knelt down in church, it came to me to turn that around. So, I prayed, "I know you love me, God, and I know you love, loving me. A feeling of rest and total peace came over me. Everything was okay. There was no more turmoil."

God's love is the path to peace, Father Rick said, "Accepting it is up to us."

Priests experience turmoil, Father Rick says, and they are better priests for it.. He said his good friend Father Don Shane once introduced the two of them at a session as "Ding bats and Dirt Balls." Priests sometimes forget they are human beings and hold themselves up to an impossibly hard standard. "All any of us (priest or lay person) have to do," he said, "is learn to love ourselves just as we are, because that is how God loves us."

Father Rick said he asked Father Shane to give the homily at his funeral because he wanted "someone who could tell nice lies really easy."

The last few years Father Rick has dealt with heart disease. The last few months all that kept him alive is the drug Dobutomine The side effects had become intolerable, so he made the decision he will no longer take the drug. "I know my Doctor, Jeff Knerl, didn't want me to make that decision. He even invited me to move in with his family," he said, "But I decided it was time. I no longer have the strength to help people. I'm just too tired. When married people tell me they're having difficulties, I just want to say, 'Grow up!'"

Thus, with sadness, serenity and humor, the last weeks of his life he seemed to be standing outside of himself, watching what was happening to his body, giving a blow by blow description to anyone interested, patiently waiting to, as he said, "cross the river." He's taking with him a myriad of special messages from people on earth to give to their loved ones in Heaven, and even as he prepared to leave, he had a sense of happiness and excitement about those he would soon see.

Those of us standing on this side of the river will experience great loss. But we will also feel great happiness, because even as he fades away from us he will be arriving at the "other side" and a joyous outcry will rise up from those waiting to greet him.

We are sure they will be waiting, because he told us so.

Father Rick Arkfeld, has finally gone home.

CHAPTER 2

Counting Our Blessings

"There's two ways of spreading light: Either to be the candle, or the mirror that reflects it." Edith Wharton

So much of what I have learned about life has come from the people about whom I have written. They have taught me, through laughter and tears, how to transcend life's difficulties with grace and dignity and wisdom and wit. The readers seemed to especially appreciate these columns. Thus, I share them with you.

Celebrating Our "And Yets......"

Thanksgiving is upon us. It is time to celebrate our "And yets...." And put our "If onlys..." behind us. What am I talking about? Just this.

In Arthur Gordon's book, "A Touch of Wonder," he wrote an essay on "The Way of Acceptance." In it he discussed the devastation we cause in our lives when we berate ourselves and others about past decisions or actions which we can no longer DO anything about. And the wondrous wisdom of accepting what has happened, and getting on with our lives. We waste time on "If onlys.." he said, when we should be concentrating on "And yets..."

Life is full of "If onlys..." We've all had them.

After Kip and I were married we went to Fort Collins, Colorado, so that Kip could go to what was then the Colorado Aggies. We loved Colorado and seriously considered buying a farm at the edge of town and staying there.

Our roots called to us, however, so we returned to Northeast Nebraska, and have never looked back. Well, almost never. Sometimes when we visit Fort Collins and view the tract of land that we almost bought we indulge in a brief "If only..."

Standing on that very parcel of land now is a major hotel, a shopping center and a golf course.

But we follow the brief "if only.." with a heart felt "And yet..." We came home to enjoy enriching relationships with relatives and good friends, a progressive small town filled with caring people, good schools, a golf course to live for, and a life style that suits us both perfectly. We have truly never been sorry. We are content.

An example Gordon uses in his essay is of a skydiver whose parachute failed to open on his nineteenth jump. He slammed into a dry lake bed at sixty miles an hour. He was told he'd never leave a hospital bed, and he sank into deep despair.

In the hospital, however, he had frequent visits from another patient, a man whose spinal cord had been severed in an automobile accident. This man would never walk, in fact, never move a finger again, but he was always cheerful.

"I certainly don't recommend my situation to anyone," he would say, "and yet I can read, I can listen to music, I can talk to people...."

Those two words "And yet..." shift the focus from what has been lost to what remains—and to what may still be gained. They gave hope to the skydiver. He came through his ordeal and today walks without a limp.

Acceptance doesn't mean apathy, says Gordon. Apathy paralyzes the will-to-action; acceptance frees it by relieving it of impossible burdens.

Neither does acceptance of who we are mean we wouldn't like a few things to be different. It only means we understand the futility of pursuing goals we can't reach.

So we set possible goals. I, for instance, would like to be a soprano, and tall, and to be able to eat everything and not gain a pound. None of those objectives are within my reach. So I accept being short , an alto, and perpetual dieter.

In fact, I rather enjoy it.

The serenity prayer says it all. We pray that the Lord grant us the strength to change things that need changing, the courage to accept things that cannot be changed, and the wisdom to know the difference.

Agreeing to Disagree
Appreciating the Grains of Sand in our Lives

The argument was about a candidate for election. Nose to nose combat between long time friends. Words flew, tempers raged. No one would believe that the next time you see these characters they'll be sitting down for a cup of coffee at the local restaurant amiably discussing the weather, or golf, or Kuwait, or Haiti, or, although they've gotten pretty tired of this subject, O.J. No political candidate, no matter how avidly supported, is going to break up this friendship. Never has. Never will.

They have come to understand, through the years, that there are a number of things on which they'll disagree. Vehemently. So they agree to disagree, getting some kind a perverse pleasure out of it. But there are so many reasons they like each other, that they are able to rise above the disagreeable periods.

It is difficult to come to grips with the fact that people have a right to be different than we prefer them to be. They perceive life differently than we want them to, they laugh at different things, they handle grief in a different manner, and may even have an allegiance to a different political party.

So they annoy us, especially this time of year, when we are in the heat of political battles. Some one may come to your mind even as you read.

It's not just in the political arena. There are some people who will annoy us always, simply because their personality clashes with ours. No fault of theirs, no fault of ours. Maybe we're messy. (!) Maybe they're neat. Maybe we're extroverts who process our thoughts by spewing them forth for all who want to listen and many who don't. Or maybe we are introverts who process internally and long for a quiet time so we can just sit quietly and contentedly and think things through.

Life has been much easier for me, much less complicated and infuriating, since I've grasped that people will be who they are, because that's who they are, and they have no choice. I accept that, because. Actually, I have no choice either.

And it's a good thing. Every group, every board, every committee, needs people with different personalities on it, people who annoy each other. They need the dreamers and schemers and creative types, and they need the practical people who say, "but are we covered by insurance when we do that?"

They need people to discuss and compromise and, yes, argue things out, in order to hammer out the best decision. Much like an oyster needs to be irritated by a grain of sand in order to produce a pearl.

You've realized by now that this is not a column about politics, it is a column about benevolently accepting differences in other people, differences we can't do anything about in any case, and, going one step further, even learning to appreciate them.

I am a morning person, a rise and shine and give God the glory, glory kind of a person, and I annoy people who aren't. Kip, for instance.

I have friends and relatives who don't even want to talk until they've had their first cup of coffee, who become alert at noon, and bloom during the evening hours, when I am ensconced on my couch taking a nap so I can make it to bed.

I'm convinced, be it nature or nurture, our behavior is somehow ingrained in our very being. To quote Henry David Thoreau," if a man does not keep pace with his companions, perhaps it is because he hears a different drummer. Let him step to the music which he hears, no matter how measured or far away."

There are people who's drummer beats in double time. They survive and thrive on one speed, and that's fast—full speed ahead. High powered people who work hard and play hard, and sometimes die young. But when they do—they've crammed a lot of living into their lives. A quote once given me in a sonorous Irish brogue by our friend, Gee O'Gara, who lives in California, but has never been far from the Old Sod, describes this type. "I'd rather be a shooting star for five seconds, than a lamp post for eternity."

Other folks worry about these people, and are always telling them to slow down. Of course, they usually tell them to slow down after they've gotten them to agree to serve on a committee, or make a speech, or paint the church, or some such thing. They are sincere about getting this person to slow down, but only if it doesn't affect what that person is doing for them, personally.

You can tell the beat of someone's drummer as they walk down the street. Some step out to march time, purposefully walking, almost running, to what we can only assume is an important destination. All New Yorkers march like this, and if they can't, they have to move somewhere else.

Others walk as if there's a waltz in their heads, gazing about them, taking in the sights as they go.

In between are the rest of us, sometimes marching, sometimes waltzing, moving to the beat of our own drummer, peculiar though that may be.

My brother, Vince Rossiter, was a true workaholic, as was my father, Emmett, before him. Always advocating for some worthy cause, they worked, truly, from early morning to late at night. I have a wee bit of that drummer in my own head.

The difference was if you got my brother on vacation, he became an instant sludge. I can do that too. But Vincent knew how to vacate better than anyone I've ever known. My Dad never did. We'd leave home on Wednesday for a week's vacation, and be back on the next Friday. Something always came up. We had phones in our bathrooms. That's probably why Dad died at 63 and Vince, with the help of his healthy-food-conscious wife, Rhea, lived till he was 75.

I'm just musing here, sharing some personal insights, as always, hoping to help us look at people who annoy us in a new light, and appreciate them for the grain of sand they just might be.

Smelling the Lilacs
with a Cactus Friend

To smell the lilacs, one must take advantage of a brief window of opportunity. Lilacs bloom when they please, and they're gone—just like that. They don't wait around. Every year I try to go with a group of good friends to smell the lilacs at Lewis and Clark Lake. It's a soul-satisfying experience. Some years, however, we are too busy, and we get there too late. When that happens, we know we better slow down.

It's the same with people. Sometimes we don't get to see the people we love because we just don't make the time. We mean to, but we don't. We know who these people are because we find ourselves writing Christmas cards to them year after year and saying, "Let's get together this year," and we mean it, but we don't do it.

These are people whom we yearn to spend time with, family members, army buddies, school friends, or anyone who's had a positive impact on our lives. But we just don't seem to get around to seeing them.

It's time to get around to it.

Pick up our phones. Make a date.

Have I put this strongly enough?

It's important to gather up your siblings and your friends and do a little hugging, because in a blink of an eye, the opportunity to do this is gone. We think we have all the time in the world. We think our siblings and friends will live for ever.

They won't. Mine didn't.

We need not live our lives always afraid that people we love are going to up and die. That would be far too depressing. We should, however, understand it's a possibility.

When that happens, we need to be able say, "I'm so glad we spent time together last summer." Not, "I wish we had..."

Years ago, one January morning, Kip said to me, "I've got a hunch we should fly out to Mesa and see Dad." So we did. Kip's Dad was to celebrate his 95 birthday on January 15. We were planning one whing-dilly of a celebration, but it was to be in Nebraska in the Spring. We had compiled a guest list of his many friends, and I was working on the program, under the vigilant eye of Dad's second wife Grace.

Then Kip got this sudden notion we should spend his actual birthday with him, and we did. We had a great time.

Dad didn't make it till spring. See what I mean?

Big deal, you might say, he was 95.

This past month, my friends, a niece and a nephew of ours (54 and 49 respectively) had heart attacks. They are doing fine, but it fills one with a sense of urgency. It makes us realize we can't always wait until Spring.

I'm not trying to be depressing, just encouraging all of us to slow down long enough to do a little hugging with our cactus friends. It's a stress relieving activity, good for our hearts, and for all the rest of us.

Who are cactus friends? I will explain.

It's my theory that the people in our lives resemble flowers. There are the friends who are like African Violets. They take a lot of tending, and won't hang around if you don't do things just their way. Some people are good with African Violets and think they are worth the trouble. I am not.

Next come the philodendron-like friends who need some care, but are still there for us even if we neglect them a little. We love them for their loyalty and their stamina, so we make sure to give them the care they need. An occasional card or letter, a phone call, a lunch along the way, and philodendrons flourish and add much beauty to our lives. They are good friends.

The very best, however, are the cactus friends. We may not see them for years, but our friendship never changes. They uplift our spirits and gentle our hearts. They are GOOD for us, and we are good for them.

Often they are relatives, who neglect us as much as we do them. Should we need them, however, they'd be by our side in a heart beat. These can also be friends from the past with whom we've experienced life in a special way, thus forming an unbreakable bond.

A cactus friend can also be a new friend, one we know instinctively is worth making an old friend out of. Rare occurrence, but it happens.

Cactus friends are all soul mates. Friends who love us in spite of ourselves.

If we are very lucky, these friends live near us, even in our house.

They are someone we just think about and it makes us smile.

However, we get busy, and they get busy, and we don't get to see them as much as we'd like to—as much as we NEED to.

So it behooves us, occasionally, to think about the lesson we learn from the lilacs, which is they don't wait around to be smelled.

Transcending Our Evil Twin

(1996—The year of Nebraska's one humiliating defeat)

I have an insightful (?) point to make about the similarity between controlling diabetes and winning football games.

Motivational types always look for an illustrative mental imagery handout to make a point. I use my "Evil Twin" theory. It suggests that people such as you and me, who are usually nice, certainly talented, and think positively about themselves and others most of the time, occasionally become over-wrought, testy, and out of control. Something upsets us, we lose perspective, and our ability to perform normally is dramatically affected. It's then our internal Evil Twin takes over, and we become unpleasant, to say the least. We need someone to vent to, some way to transcend our selves, some way to get us out of this rotten, self-defeating mood.

The connection of Kip's borderline diabetes (and any other debilitating life experience) and Nebraska's stunning loss to Arizona, is elementary, dear reader. Overcoming adversity, in life or on the playing field, boils down to confidence, attitude and determination. And that is something that happens in our heads.

A booklet about diabetes, puts it this way.

"Belief about ourselves dramatically affects our behavior. We all give ourselves messages all the time." Too often, these messages are negative: "I'm too lazy." "I'm too fat." "I should have done a better job." "I can't do that." "I can't stand this." "I'm going to lose."

These are the "killer phrases" from our Evil Twin. They erode self esteem and make us less effective, less happy, less able to take care of ourselves, and less able to call on our own resources to heal ourselves, whether of a disease of the body, or a disease of the mind.

The article says we need to practice giving ourselves positive affirmations—telling ourselves we are capable, in fact, we are darned good. We deserve happiness, praise, love, and victory. We can take control of a situation and do well. We can. We can. We can.

If we lose faith in ourselves, that isn't going to happen. For instance, everyone knew Nebraska would beat Arizona. Except, it seems, Arizona. Watching in our living rooms, we were sure Nebraska would turn it around. Positive. It was only on the last incongruous fumble that we began to understand that the team we were watching wasn't our determined, confident team. They'd been replaced by their evil twins. Once they quit believing in themselves, they were done. Something-perhaps a psychological factor we may never understand—happened to those magnificent athletes. They lost confidence in themselves and each other.

Maybe, as suggested by sports commentators, one factor was that we, the fans, have gotten too blasé, too demanding, and no longer display the wild enthusiasm needed to inspire such a team.

Because, you see, those boys didn't lose their ability, they lost their mental acuity, concentration, and their belief in themselves.

A stunning disappointment to team, coaches and fans, it might be the wake up call we all need to do what we have to do to pick ourselves up, dust ourselves off, and start all over again. Because this happens. It happens in the pros, to individuals and to teams at every level. We've seen it happen at state tournaments, in our own gymnasiums and on our playing fields. A talented team loses it, while a demonstrably less talented team catches fire.

Coaches look for magic words to change the situation, but sometimes the problem is so deep in the psyche they can't get to it. And fans, an integral part their success, get morose and grumbly just when they should be screaming encouragement.

Coaches sometimes do dramatic and outrageous things, fight with officials, get penalized, even get kicked out of the game, to light a fire under their team. Sometimes it works. Sometimes it doesn't.

The people seated around our TV wondered what would happen if Osbourn would flip out and run up and down the field screaming like a banshee. I'll bet in his heart of hearts he wanted to. He could no more do that than he could fly, given his personality.

The good news is that evil twins can be banished. Our body and our mind have remarkable ability to heal themselves if we get the help we need, nurture ourselves and keep a positive perspective.

Therefore, the greatest belief we can cultivate is HOPE. We do that by hanging out with positive people, reading positive books, thinking positively, and avoiding the whimpy whiners of the world., Then we're on the way to winning our game, whatever that might be.

We also need our loved ones (our fans) to literally and figuratively race up and down the sidelines urging us on, screaming like banshees.

Go Kip Go!!

Go June Go!!!

Go Nebraska Go!!!!

Contemplating Change!!

For those born before the forties.

(Whatever your age, this will give you a few chuckles.)

Consider the changes we have witnessed....

Although this was written for people born before the forties, no matter what your age, it will give you a few chuckles.

We were born before television, before penicillin, before polio shots, frozen foods, contact lenses, Frisbees and the Pill.

We were born before radar, credit cards, split atoms, laser beams and ball point pens, before panty-hose, dishwashers, clothes' dryers, electric blankets, air conditioners, drip-dry clothes—and before man walked on the moon.

We got married first and then lived together. How quaint can you be?

In our time, closets were for clothes, not for "coming out of." Bunnies were small rabbits and rabbits were not Volkswagons. Designer Jeans were scheming girls named Jean, or Jeanne, and having a meaningful relationship meant getting along well with our cousins.

We thought fast food was what you ate during Lent, and outer Space was the back of the Riviera Theater.

We were born before house-husbands, gay rights, computer dating, dual careers or computer marriages. We were born before day-care centers, group therapy and nursing homes. We never heard of FM radio, tape decks, electric typewriters, artificial hearts, word processors, or guys wearing ear rings. For us, time-sharing meant togetherness—not computers or condominiums: a "chip" meant a piece of wood; hardware meant hardware, and software wasn't even a word.

In 1940 "Made in Japan" did not imply quality, and "making out" referred to how you did on your exam. Pizzas, MacDonalds and instant coffee were unheard of.

We hit the scene when there were 5¢ and 10¢ stores where you bought things for five and ten cents. Ice cream cones sold for a nickel or a dime. For one nickel you could ride a street car (trolley), make a phone call, buy a Pepsi, or enough stamps to mail one letter and two postcards. You could buy a new Chevy Coupe for $600., but who could afford one; a pity too, because gas was 11¢ a gallon.

In our day, cigarette smoking was fashionable, grass was mowed, Coke was a drink and Pot was something you cooked in. Rock music was Grandma's lullaby, and AIDS were helpers in the Principal's office.

We were certainly not born before the difference between the sexes was discovered, but we were surely born before the sex change; we made do with what we had, and we were the last generations that seemed to think you needed a husband to have a baby!

No wonder we are so confused and there is such a generation gap today!

But, nevertheless, we survived!

What better reason to celebrate!

Don't Lose the Things
That Money CAN'T Buy
"Read once before Christmas"

I was cleaning off my cluttered desks and a little card fell on the floor. On it was a quotation attributed to George Horace Lorimer: It read as follows:

"It's good to have money and the things that money can buy, but it is good, too, to check up once in a while and make sure that you haven't lost the things that money can't buy."

"This must be providential," I thought. What a good quote to ponder on as the Holiday season approaches when all the emphasis seems to be on buying things, when it should be on appreciating what money can't buy, families, friends, faith, freedom.

I need to ponder on this because I get carried away at Christmas in the "thing" department. I get everything bought for the family, all nice and even, and then I find one more thing that one of the kids will just love, and I get so tickled, and I buy that too, and then I have to start evening up again. .

Some times I'm the only one who's tickled. I seem to have a rare talent for picking out things I want people to want, but they don't necessarily want, if you know what I mean. If one would call that a talent. Probably not.

I used to always give my daughter Juli suits, mostly sincere blue ones, and she never wore them. I just hoped she would. Juli is a comedian, a theater person, among other things, a little wacky in a nice sort of way, as are most theater people. She's always had a secure sense of who she is. She dresses accordingly.

I asked her one time what she ever did with the suits, since I'd never seen one on her. She told me that they were all in the Doane Theater's costume department.

I've given my boys so many sweaters that they've asked me to quit. I love big, colorful sweaters, but even Bill, who lives in Colorado, says they are too hot to wear. You'd think sweaters would be perfect in Colorado.

Kip is the hard one to buy for. He doesn't want anything, bah, humbug, and he truly means that. The greatest gift I could give him would be not to BUY anything. Therefore, I go to great trouble to surprise him.

My best surprise gift was when I took all his World War II medals, wings etc, and had them put into a huge antique frame. He was overwhelmed, and pleased, and that year—for the first time in his life—he talked to our children about his war experience. That time—and maybe only that time—I was inspired.

I like to get gifts too, of course, and I don't much care what they are as long as I get to open a package. A lot of my "inner" child isn't so inner. However, what I really want from my family is to have them here, or have them call. If they aren't here, they darned well better call!!

But I digress, and I had a serious point to make here. I think. Oh yes, it is this. When it comes to presents, it IS the thought counts. If children would just give there folks a card that said, "I will clean up my room without nagging for the next year," or " I'll mow the yard every two weeks," parents would be ecstatic.

Gifts of self, gifts of prayer, gifts of home made goodies, phone calls, gifts that don't cost much but speak of the love they represent, those are the very best kind.

Now, if I can just remember that!

We're Blessed!

1995

The hills are alive with the sound of tractors, and that is music to our ears. As I write this column we've had seven days of blessed sun, glorious sun, wonderful, beautiful life-giving sun. Our farmers, who have been sitting in their tractors revving the engines for several weeks now, burst out of the starting gate (so to speak), an army of great machines beginning their planting dance. Racing mother nature, they allemande left and do-si-do through their fields and up and down the roads, almost frantic to be about their job, which they do with amazing expertise, feeding the nation and the world.

The crazy quilt landscape out our picture window changes hues even as I write, as black earth is overturned, starkly contrasting to the lush green of hay meadows and pasture ground, and strait rows of furrows come into view, designating corn planted and ready to sprout. It will change rapidly now, must change, actually, if corn is to be knee high by the fourth of July. I have watched this transformation most of my life from this little red house on the hill, and it is soothing to the soul.

I have to tell you, however, as much rain as we have had, when we were driving down the road yesterday and saw dust, we got a little worried. Dust reminds us of drought , and we never seem to be able to NOT worry about something.

However, not for long, because our resident meadow lark, sitting on the top of our highest evergreen tree, calls upon the world to rejoice. And tiny yellow finches, who make you laugh just to see them, swoop merrily about our bird feeder, color coordinating in a breathtaking way with a massive display of giant yellow tulips. The tulips much to my surprise, rose up out of the ground en masse this year, like I had planned the whole effect. I must have planted them sometime, but it had slipped my mind. And, although the yellow tulips will soon be history, yellow lilies will soon bloom, and my color co-ordination with the yellow finches, however inadvertent, will remain intact.

Sometimes, my reader friends, I tackle hard subjects, that make even me cringe, and sometimes I do travelogues, sometimes personality profiles, sometimes family updates, sometimes commentaries on life in general, and sometimes I resort to just plain foolishness.

This is none of above. It is a psalm to our country, which is the best in the world. It celebrates, specifically, the Midwest, which is the very best part of the very best country in the world. We have our problems, and terrible things happen, unbelievable things, things we can hardly take in, they upset us so. But we have ways to tackle them within the law, within our churches, within our homes.

And life-affirming things are happening all about us now. Baby critters scamper about in our meadow, the farmers are in their fields, and soon the lilacs will be in bloom. We can pray in our churches without fear. We can speak out about anything on our streets or in our papers, and nobody will stop us. We don't have famine, or war in our streets, nor do we have to worry about ground that is due any moment to shake rattle and roll. We have tornadoes, but, for the most part, we know about them and can take cover. We have problems, however, by working together, we can come up with solutions.

We are lucky folks. We are blessed.

As I watch my finches, and hear the meadow lark over the hum of the tractors working the fields, I am reminded of that, and so, I thought I would remind you too.

Have You Heard the One About.........
(The Blessing of Humor)

Have you heard the one about the grandson who told his friends,"I want to die in my sleep and at peace like Grandpa did. Not screaming and hollering like the rest of the people with him in his car."

This story is making the rounds now, and I use it only as an example. Depending upon what kind of a sense of humor you have, or where you are in life right now, you either laughed or were offended. Or both.

If you laughed, however, or even grinned, it was good for your mental and therefore physical health. Because laughter is good for what ails you. It is internal jogging, a mini-vacation.

Non-hostile laughter is best, of course, but our body just likes us to laugh. Magazines on latest diseases of interest at our house, rheumatoid arthritis and diabetes, feature in-depth articles declaring that laughter is "the best medicine for the mind, body, and spirit." Studies show, they say, that human beings can, if they choose, use laughter to counteract negative feelings, such as anger or frustration, and to combat the destructive inroads of depression and despondency caused by illness and grief. Since this is a drum I've been beating for a long time, it is gratifying to have corroborating evidence.

For instance, an article in the "Diabetes: Self Management" magazine, by Caren Goldman, states that the scientific and sociological interest in the power of humor to heal has resulted in "humor physiology" which is showing that even "small doses of merriment and mirth enhance the function of the circulatory, hormonal, nervous, immune, and respiratory systems in the body. It can also help alleviate anxiety, depression and stress."

This is good news for all those who are looking for ways to live with the emotional and physiological consequences of a chronic illness.

William F. Fry, jr. MD.., Standford Medial School, says tests show 10 seconds of belly laughter has the same ventilating and heart-strengthening results as ten minutes of rowing. Ten seconds!

We often choose friends because we laugh at the same thing. Laughers laugh at different things, and even laugh differently. They howl, guffaw, giggle or tee-hee. And there are people who can laugh inside and never crack a smile. Kip, my cattle-feeder husband, is one. How we got together I don't know, except I'm sure he laughed more before we were married. (Perhaps I should think about that.)

Juli got us front seats for a noted comedian's performance. It was hilarious. I howled and guffawed and giggled. Kip didn't even smile. It's his modus operandi. Comedians find this disconcerting. They try to get to those people. No one gets to Kip. The comedian, a friend of Juli's, came to her after the show, visibly upset. "Who was that crabby guy in the front row?" he asked. Juli said,"That's my Dad. Don't worry. He was having a good time. He just hates to show it."

Exactly! Kip said afterwards, "He was pretty good, wasn't he?"

I laugh out loud when my friend, South Dakota's famed author, Bob Karolevitz says anything in his assumed Norwegian accent. I giggle at the newspaper typos in the Reader's Digest. Could be because, without good editors, my column would be full of them.

The important point is that the evidence is in, and it's irrefutable. We need to laugh.

The question is, how do we do it?

These suggestions (comments by me) are from Patty Wooten, RN., B.S.N. C.C.R.N. president of the American Association of Therapeutic humor.

* Discover what really makes you laugh. (Hang out with people who make you laugh, go to funny movies, do things you find amusing. Having a sense of humor doesn't mean being able to tell jokes or entertain. It means being a "humor participant.")

*Be foolish. (We NEED to do something completely silly and totally non-productive occasionally. I know a person who carries red noses in her brief case for humor emergencies.) (Okay, so it's me!)

*Use your imagination. (To relieve the stress of speaking, a professor told us, "imagine the audience in pajamas." I shared that with an audience. A guy yelled, "I don't wear pajamas.")

*Recall funny events with people who shared them. (Think memories: reunions, conventions, card clubs, coffee groups)

*Trade embarrassing moments. (They can be hilarious, in retrospect. My friend, the late Marge Seim, shared a true tale told her by a dignified secretary. The secretary was taking minutes at a round table with a group of ministers. She got hot, and started to unbutton her jacket and remove it. It wasn't until she saw the shocked look on the minister's faces she remembered she wasn't wearing a jacket.)

So, be a humor participant. It will lower your blood pressure and raise your spirits. Laughter is the music of the soul.

Offer It Up

I have a theory, based on years of observation of imperfect human beings like myself, that too often we miss smelling the lilacs, and it's our own fault. I explained that to Father Rick Arkfeld one Saturday morning, weeping as if there were no tomorrow.

He, of course, understood.

It was apropos, because it was that very morning that I was not going to visit Father Rick because I had deadlines upon me. He'd been in Hartington awhile, but I'd been gone, or wildly busy, or so I thought, anyway, and I hadn't gotten around to getting in to see him. I planned to go see him soon, but it would have to wait until tomorrow—or perhaps next week.

Then I started to write something about "crossing the river" and added, as I often do, "As Father Rick Arkfeld would say."

I looked at what I'd written, turned off my computer, and went to town. I knew, somehow, that I needed to talk to Father Rick, and tomorrow wasn't going to cut it.

When I came in the door of his apartment, he looked up at me from the recliner where he spent most of his time during his last days, and said, "Where've you been? I'm dying, you know."

This time, he really was. He'd made the decision to stop taking the drug that was keeping his heart going, and death was inevitable—perhaps just in days. It was the thought that I'd put off coming to see him until it was almost too late that set me on my crying jag. I still cry when I think of what I would have missed.

Father Rick watched me with a kind of detached interest, and then said, "Why are you crying, you've always known I was going to die." I said, "I'm not crying for you, you big dummy, I'm crying for me." That's the way we talked to each other.

That's when I told him about missing the lilacs.

As we visited, I wondered aloud if he'd want me to write something for him at the end of his journey through life looking through the "window of death", just as I had at the beginning, ten years before.

"I wouldn't have asked you," he said, "but now that you've asked, I would like that." I said I'll be in next Tuesday, and he said, "I might not be here." So I came in the next morning and for several days thereafter and he talked and talked, and I listened and listened. He told me stories of his adventures on his remarkable journey, talked about the hurting people he'd helped, the miraculous ways they'd come into his life. We laughed and we cried. Flowing through these stories was always his wonder at the gift of healing God had given him that allowed him to touch so many lives, and his marvelous (although sometimes acerbic) self-deprecating humor.

I typed every thing he'd wanted me to say in a rough draft and took it in for him to read. Some of the personal stories about others I couldn't use because they were too revealing. Many of them, however, he used on his tapes and in his sermons. He is (was) the only one who could tell his stories, weaving sadness and happiness together masterfully, pausing dramatically, modulating his voice, speaking to our very souls.

He read over what I'd written, me prancing around nervously. "I haven't put the sizzle in yet," I told him, "it's just a rough draft." He said, "It's accurate, but you better work on that sizzle."

The result was the story in the Oct. 18, 1996 Catholic Voice. (On page 27.)

I couldn't go to Father Rick's funeral because of a previous engagement with our Granddaughter Abbie Jane Burney who came into the world just as Father Rick was leaving it. He'd have loved the symbolism. It was okay, because we'd said our good byes. I'd seen the lilacs, as it were.

It behooves me, now, to explain about the lilacs. Every spring, you see, I go with a group of friends to see and smell the lilacs at Lewis and Clark Lake. They are spectacular.

Or, at least, I plan to.

One has to go see the lilacs when the lilacs are ready. you know. They don't wait around. So sometimes I miss them. But when I do, I know there is something very wrong in my life.

Not getting to have my last hours with Father Rick would have been far more serious than missing the lilacs, but, in a sense, the same kind of self-imposed loss. I explained all this to Father Rick on that first visit, tears rolling down my face, trying to make him understand how sorry I was that I hadn't stopped by sooner. I told him because of his tapes he has always been with me, and I hadn't even thought that maybe I should be with him.

He looked at me thoughtfully, letting me wallow in my seemly grief, and then, with a slight grin on his face, he nodded, and smiled, and said, "It's okay, Joanie. You are here now. Things happen when they should happen." He had, in essence, accepted my apology, which was, we both realized, not so much to him, as to myself.

Mostly, we joshed one another. Twice in a row he sent me home unceremoniously because he HAD to go to the bathroom. Another time, sensing I might be staying too long again, I said to him, "Aren't you going to have to go to the bathroom pretty soon."

He said, "Don't worry, I'll let you know."

The last time I saw him he razed me about something, and I said, "I'm going to do a personal column about you too, you know. Then I can tell the readers whatever I want to."

And Father Rick said, suddenly serious, "Don't forget to tell them about taking time to smell the lilacs."

The Swing

Umpteen years ago, when I was about six years old, my father, Emmett W. Rossiter, took my little sister Anne and me to visit the farm of Dwight W. Burney, Sr. a prominent Cedar County cattle feeder as well as a Senator in the Nebraska Legislature. Dad had just bought the Bank of Hartington and was making contacts.

Kip and I have two different versions of what happened that fateful day.

Kip says that it was the very day of that visit (at six years old, mind you) that I took one look at him and set my sights on marrying him.

Not true. I remember, vaguely, seeing an uppity older "man" of eleven, but what I really fell in love with was the swing in the Burney yard. On it's third generation of Burneys when I saw it at six years old, it was built on it's own sturdy steel frame, and consisted of two bench-like seats facing each other. A perfect place for adults to sit across from each other, swing and visit, and a more than perfect place for kids. I loved that swing.

Many a time, after Kip and I were married, I sat in that swing with one kid or other and visited with Grandma Edna. When we'd go to visit

Grandpa and Grandma, the first place our kids would head would be to The Swing.

When Wid and Virginia moved to the big house, the swing continued to be a gathering spot. Getting old, a little rusty, a little the worse for wear, it still had a mystique. It was a place where problems were discussed and worked out, a focal point for picnics and celebrations.

In later years, after Wid died and Virginia went into the nursing home, and nobody used the swing any more, it deteriorated pitifully.

One day, when Wid's son Travis was up for a visit, I voiced my concern about the dilapidated old swing, and waxed eloquent about the "old days." "You want that swing, it's yours," he said, "we'll never use it or fix it up."

I couldn't believe my ears. I had taken me only until I was 18 year old to land Kip. It's taken a whole whale of a lot longer to land that swing. Kip and I went up to check it out. The boards were all rotted, the steel frame rusted. Could it be resurrected? The two of us put the carcass of the beloved old swing in the pick up, and hauled it to town to the Carhart Lumber Co. hospital.

Could it be resurrected!! If you could look out our picture window you would do what I do, just grin. There sits that old swing, triumphantly sporting a bright coat of red on its steel frame, holding up newly built seats of pristine white. It's a beauty.

When everything in the world seems to have gone awry--when "politics as usual" begins to make me sick to my stomach--when bad things happen to good people, and I hurt so much for them I could cry and never stop--when I simply want to feel good about life--I can now head for The Swing.

I like to think ghosts of all the Burney's of by-gone years will hover about, infusing whoever swings there with a little of the wisdom and humor they shared so generously in their days on earth.

I know generations to come will swing in that swing because they already have. Wid's daughter Pat's son Jeff's two children, beautiful little people, two and three years old, had a go at it just this week. They loved it! These two tiny creatures, Candy and Travis Kim, are our great, great nephew and niece. They are the seventh generation to enjoy the mystique of the swing.

You'd love it too. Come on by. We'll pour us a glass of lemonade and have a swinging time!

CHAPTER THREE

Family and Friends

The following columns I share because they are about things that happened in yesteryear, in my family, or in my extended family, along with things that have happened since my last books were published that changed my life forever in many wondrous ways.

As an opening, therefore, I share with you the poem my daughter Juli gave me years ago. It describes ALL my various families. It will describe yours too.

You will love it, and use it over and over, as I have.

A Family of Friends

You'll find there's a family of friends sitting here
A warm group of minds and of hearts,
With some of us clever and some of us not,
Most time's you can't tell us apart!
There's one who is cranky
and one who is shy
and one who is really uncouth.
And just when you think you've discovered who's who
You really uncover the truth.
The truth is, we're all just a little of each,
A group of imperfects are we,
And sometimes I might criticize them to you,
But don't ever knock them to me.
'Cause the one thing that keeps us together for life,
No matter how far we're apart,
Is our love for each other, this family of friends,
This warm group of minds and of hearts.

(by Judith Bond)

Singing in the Old Cadillac
(The Golden Days of Yore)

My favorite memories of my Mom and Dad revolve around music. Long summer evenings passed gently with Mom at the grand piano and Dad and his friend Edgar Hoar enthusiastically harmonizing on songs that were golden oldies even then, such as My Wild Irish Rose, and There's A Long Long Trail A Winding. The music wafted out open windows and doors (no air conditioning then) and onto the front porch where my little sister Anne and I gathered with our motley array of friends. Sometimes we'd join in the singing, adding enthusiastic little girl voices, and Grandma Welch sang too, a warbling soprano. It was an interesting mix. In later years, I got to be the pianist, and Mom would sing along. A big moment for me.

We also sang when we took the "Ride," every Sunday afternoon (capitalized because it was that important). Mom would holler, "It's time for the Ride," and we'd come running from up a tree or out in the shed or down the street, and climb into a 1928 Cadillac Convertible, which was Dad's pride and joy.

Top down we'd head out, our destination the country roads covering the rolling hills of Cedar County. The "Riders" were Mom and Dad and Anne and I and the aforementioned Grandma Welch, a crusty little woman, one of the first woman editors in Nebraska.

Grandma was a memory in and of herself. She drank her whisky neat, and was an expert at everything; sewing, gardening, cooking and writing. She lived with us twelve years, and—although we didn't appreciate it at the time—she enriched our lives.

Dad purchased the Cadillac after the City of Omaha retired it from duties as the official parade car. He told us Presidents road down Dodge street in the back seat of that car, and we believed him, which caused trouble, because than we had to argue about who was sitting where the President sat.

We loved the singing. We prided ourselves on knowing all the verses of My Darling Clementine. And harmonize! Well, let me tell you. Momma did sang alto, and Daddy sang tenor, and the rest of us joined right in there. That wasn't all. It was also thrilling, because Dad drove over hills so fast our tummies leaped up in a most satisfactory way, and if a hapless rabbit wandered in the beam of headlights, which they always seemed to do, we'd chase it down the road, Dad whooping and hollering, Mom saying, "Now Emmett!!"

We must have been a sight that made people smile, driving down the road singing and laughing. At least we are in my mind's eye. What a wonderful memory.

It was, I'm sure, what we now call "quality" time.

* * * * * * * * * *

Every Child Needs a Hidden Paradise!

For the first 13 years of my life our family spent every summer at Long Pine, Nebraska's, Hidden Paradise Resort. It nestles in a lovely valley with an ice cold creek meandering through it, and is completely hidden until one drives down a canyon road and finds it there, midst the tree covered mountains.

(Okay, so they are only "mountains" to little kids.)

My sister Anne and I were allowed to roam the "mountains" at will. We climbed to the top of the canyon to and hollered, and waited for the echoes to respond. They did. Although sometimes it was just our older siblings yelling back.

It was the wickedly cold creek, however, that was the center of our lives. Once we got in and got acclimated to the water, we stayed. Mom delivered peanut butter and jelly sandwiches to the creek's edge. We'd make a rock dam in the creek and watch polly wogs turn into frogs. We'd take patched inner tubes as far as we could go up the creek, and ride them down. It was a great ride, even though we had to portage over the shallow spots to avoid wearing out the bottoms of our bathing suits on the rocks. Nobody ever worried about our safety. On the contrary, they seemed glad to have us out of their hair.

Our cottage was a long room with a huge stone fire place on one end (perfect for roasting marshmallows and wieners) and a stark dressing room on the other. Off to the side was a tiny kitchen, with an equally tiny two burner kerosene stove. A long screened-in porch fronted the cottage, and every one slept in cots that ringed the entire porch, covered with khaki "army" blankets. We slept in fresh pine-smelling air, with the background music of the rustling trees and the gurgling creek.

Except on the weekends. Then we were lulled (?) to sleep by the dance bands playing at the open Pavilion just across the creek. Our three older sisters went dancing. One more year, I'd have gotten to go. That may be why we stopped going.

What was really exciting was when a storm came up. We dashed madly around the porch, standing on cots to roll down heavy canvas shades for protection.

It was Heaven for two little girls, but a rugged existence for Mom. We kept things cool in an ice box, got water from an outside pump, and our bathroom facility, a three-hole out-house, was several hundred feet away, around a bend.

Mom left modern homes to have all this fun, cooked huge meals for constant company on that two burner kerosene stove, washed clothes on a wash board in huge tub, carried water and plucked chickens. No where is it recorded how much fun she had.

Mom saw to our basic needs, warned us about getting lost and poison ivy, but then she left us to our own devices, a tactic John Rosemond would applaud heartily, and we were glad. As free as the birds, we taught ourselves to swim in the deep holes in the creek. We discovered for ourselves why we should stay away from poison ivy, and when we got lost trying to follow a mother cat to her kittens, we found our way home. We gained wisdom and confidence from being allowed to experience the consequences of our own actions.

Parents can still give children this kind of freedom in places like Hidden Paradise, I think, and many small towns, like ours, where a whole village still does help raise the children. Living on a farm is a great place to raise kids. Chores are a given, and the children have as their play ground the wide open spaces.

The child advocates are saying many parents now are too protective. For good reason, in some cases, because we must protect children from life-threatening situations. But in any other kind of situation, if we always pick our children up when they fall, always take their side, we rob them of the opportunity to pick themselves up, to learn to solve their own problems. Our gut feeling is that we don't want them to hurt. Mostly, we don't want us to hurt. Parenting is not a popularity contest. If you're not popular with your children, it probably means you're doing your job. A little hurt now saves a huge hurt later.

I wish every child could experience the freedom we had at Hidden Paradise. After all these years, I can still smell the fresh air, hear the whistling pines and the gurgling creek, and feel the excitement that came with the first clap of distant thunder warning of an incoming storm.

Kip and His B-17

"Look at what's flying over us!" Kip shouted just as I was getting ready to make my most spectacular putt of the day.

I was annoyed. Couldn't he see that I was concentrating?

But I looked.

The putt was forgotten. The sight I saw made the world stand still for a few minutes. It was a B-17. The Flying Fortress. The kind of plane Kip flew in World War II. It was a beauty. I saluted, tears in my eyes.

Memories flooded in. This was the plane that a dark good looking young man my folks called "the wild Burney boy" buzzed the main street of Hartington with, in the early forties when he was in training at Sioux City Air Force Base.

Kip claims he never really "buzzed" Hartington, though he may have flown over it a time or two. He admits, however, buzzing a field where his father and the neighbors were threshing, startling men and horses alike.

"We weren't as low as they thought we were," he says now, but the threshing crew claim the plane came over the hill just a few feet over their heads. It was a sight they'd never forget, and although they fussed, it was with pride, because the pilot was the farm kid that not too long ago had been stacking hay right beside them..

Can you believe it, at 19 years of age, Kip flew that plane to war, the head pilot with a crew of "older men" (the oldest was 21) who have remained life-long friends.

After training in Sioux City, Kip was sent to Lincoln where he picked up his crew to head for Europe. Fresh in mind was the story Jean Cook told a few weeks ago about how her Charlie and Kip, both pilots, promised Jean they would fly down A Street in Lincoln blinking their lights when they left for Europe. They did, and Jean watched them go, weeping. Then she called Kip's folks to say he was on his way. To war!! Can you imagine how they must have felt?

The plane that flew over us as we played golf on the Sunland Golf Course in Mesa is called Sentimental Journey. It is housed at the Falcon Air Base in Mesa, a favorite among a collection of World War II planes exhibited here.

Kip's been there a number of times, patting the plane like an old friend, going through it with children who have shown up for brief visits, and with almost perfect Kate, our 11 year old Granddaughter. What a living history lesson it has been for our family, going through that plane with their dad, the old warrior who actually flew it.

Kip is fond of the plane. The men who flew the B-17, according to historians, all had a great fondness for it, because no matter how badly it got shot up, they could almost always fly it home.

There are scrapbooks full of photos of B-17s at the exhibit which show planes that had been shot to smithereens. Kip pointed out the ones that resembled his plane after it got hit. It makes one shudder.

That's why I also have a great fondness for the B-17, and why seeing it is an emotional experience. Because on Kip's 19th mission his plane got blown full of holes, and so did Kip's arm, a flight vest and medicine kit protecting his chest. He and his crew got a bunch of medals for bringing the limping plane home. He down-plays this because, he says, "What choice did we have?"

The B-17, built by Boeing, one of the oldest Aircraft Manufacturers in the country, went through several developmental stages, and it was the B-17 G that Kip flew. When it came down the assembly line, a long range bomber that Boeing called the "Aerial Battle Cruiser," it had "gun blisters every where you looked." A newsman nicknamed it "The Flying Fortress." The name stuck. The planes were given colorful names, some of them to become famous, such as Suzy Q, Blood and Memphis Belle. Kip's plane was called KwiturBitchen.

The first B-17 G flew on May 21, 1943, and on July 29, 1945, the last of the 8,680 B-17 Gs rolled off the assembly line. These planes saw action in three wars after World War Two. The Korean war, Israel's war in 1948, and the Viet Nam war, when a couple of all Black B-17Gs were used to drop agents into North Viet Nam.

But as far as Kip's concerned, the B-17 WON World War II. We don't argue.

Most of the time, I live in today. I believe it's best. But sometimes memories of yesterday need to be indulged in because they enrich today with a special light. You may not have a B-17 in your memory file, although some of you do, but you do have poignant, sad and happy memories to share, and they will help the children in your life better understand their roots, while also giving them a foundation on which to build memories of their own.

The Rossiter Family Reunion—1992
(With Great Ideas for Yours!)

If you are thinking about having a reunion, I respectfully suggest you get with it. We started talking about our reunion three years ago when my brother Vince and brother-in-law John Stockwell were still alive. Nobody would have enjoyed this gathering of the clan more than those two characters. They didn't stick around for it. They died.

They were sorely missed. We could just as well have done it when they were around. Now, however, is better than never.

Since I'm a pro, here are some suggestions for you when you plan your reunion:

Get reservations early for things like an eating place, a shelter house, motel and hotel rooms.

Get everything in writing. Mistakes happen, and it's frustrating. If you don't think so, visit with Jeanene Kuehn, who just organized a Miller reunion and found out the rooms she thought she had booked were not available.

Put each branch of the family in a different color T-shirt. This is great fun and provides instant recognition. The Milleas, who are Irish as Paddy's pig, were all in green. The V.E.Rossiter Sr. family, were in Rhea's favorite color, yellow. Lawrence's family was in aqua. The Stockwells were in red. Every color of the rainbow was represented on the families, and from the well over six footers, to the toddlers with T-shirts hanging to their knees, you knew where each person belonged by the color of his shirt.

We were going to put our official family crest on our T-shirts. I brought one back from Ireland, but it has the ugliest alligator on it you've ever seen. We opted for a shamrock, with the Rossiter motto "Boldly and Faithfully" on the front, and our own family name on the back.

We borrowed the idea of the t-shirts from the Peitz family. They had their reunion a few years back. Jack and Therese (Peitz) Thielen, our beloved friends, came to visit us with their whole clan, all dressed in blue T-shirts. They were adorable.

Another great idea, my sister Anne's, was to compile everyone's family tree in a booklet. Because of our genetic procrastination problem, this wasn't easy, but Anne persevered, phoned, wrote, and heckled until she got it done. It will be great to have this booklet.

An idea we didn't carry out, but should have, was cousin Rossiter Mullaney's. He suggested each family member write down memories which I, being the writer person, could then compile into a booklet. I was willing. Letters went out again.

Everybody liked the idea, but the only person I got written memories from was Ross.

Ross is 6 ft four inches tall, a retired F.B.I. man, and he's used to having people follow his suggestions. I tried to comfort him with the idea that we would do the memories spontaneously the night of the dinner, and we'd video tape. This would have the double benefit of fleshing out memories of those who have gone to that great reunion in the sky, while also capturing us in living color.

He wasn't much mollified, saying crankily he thought that I, at least, would have written my memories, being a writer and all.

With a flash of brilliance I said "I have"—and I presented him with two of my books. Somehow or other, he didn't realize I'd compiled my columns, OOPS, I mean, "memories," into book form.

He must not have been among the lucky relatives I gave them to at Christmas time.

It was an extraordinary experience. I had a wonderful time, and everyone else seemed to also, with the possible exception of some of the young adult cousins, who'd been coerced into coming, and occasionally looked as if they wondered why.

Personally, I instantly bonded with all of them, especially relatives who were old friends and remain so even though we hadn't seen each other for years.

When the last ones left, the Mullaneys and the Sadaros, I was sad. Bereft, almost. It was as if I'd been reading a very good book, and I didn't want it to end.

I realized, however, when Yvette called from the Airplane on her way back to California to tell me about a Rossiter relative she'd met in the Air Port, that it wasn't the end, it was another beginning.

You see, dear readers, renewing friendships with long lost relatives is just one of the many bonuses in this Reunion business.

Try it, you'll like it. (Don't wait too long!)

"You're Talking to a Man Who's 93 Years Old"

When Kip's dad was 93 years old, we invited him to dinner. We served, as we often do, prime rib. We are after all, as you might know, cattle feeders.

Dad Burney ate with relish, and I was pleased, until I noticed he was cutting a piece of beef and then a piece of fat, and eating them together. A piece of fat!

I kept my silence for 30 seconds or so, and then said to him, "Dad, you shouldn't really be eating that fat, it's not good for you."

He just grinned, and replied, "Joanie, you're talking to a man who is 93 years old."

The above exchange shows you that some people are not adversely affected by fat, I think it's genetic. But also, it shows that cattle feeders are concerned about folks who are adversely affected.

That's why the succulent chubby, square animals of yore, fed corn till their beef was marbled with fat, have disappeared. Beef and pork feeders are breeding ugly (in my way of thinking) critters who are long and lean and almost devoid of fat. It was a shock when the first long, skinny critter won a purple ribbon in the 4-H contest at our Cedar County Fair. Kip explained, "This is the way we have to go."

Now, except for prime rib, you'd be hard put to find marbling in beef. And by the time it's trimmed, fat is almost nonexistent.

So, it is gratifying to me that studies in my multitude of health newsletters, say that eating three ounces of beef is the same as eating three ounces of pork or chicken, and these sources of protein, the consummate building block, are important to your diet. Their concern is too many people, especially the elderly, are developing protein deficiencies because of over-concern about eating meat.

Personal experience tells me this is true. When I was working on bringing my cholesterol down (which is fine now, thank you very much) I cut out anything that hinted of fat, including beef. But I found I couldn't do without beef. I felt weak. So I cut down, ate sensible amounts, and—it turns out—I was right!

I have relatives and friends who are vegetarians, and I understand—except when one lectures me on the perils of eating meat. I never argue, even with studies to back me up, because it's like arguing about religion. Most ,however, just politely decline my meat dish, and load up with potatoes, vegetables, fruit, and dessert, of which, like every good farmwife, I serve commodious amounts.

I've learned other comforting things from my Wellness letters, and some not so comforting. In the Harvard Heart Letter, July, 1966, for instance, it says that short stature is NOT a risk for heart disease. Wonderful news.

Not so comforting, in the April University of California of Berkeley Wellness Letter, confirmed by the June Harvard Heart Letter, it says there is "No Support for Beta Carotene Supplements." which I have faithfully taking as a necessary anti-oxidant for years. In fact, they quote a study in Finland, published in 1994, which found beta carotene supplements increased risk of lung cancer for smokers. That startled me, until I remembered I didn't smoke.

The newsletters tell you about a study that's garnered major headlines, and then tell you it's flaws. They keep one cynical.

I didn't mean to take so many health newsletters. They are an overkill. I got suckered in with slick advertising and their offer of the first copy, containing invaluable information, free. I think, why not? Then in just a few days (it seems) I'm getting a past due bill for the health letters I "subscribed" too. Of course, I pay.

I suspect , however. I'd feel healthier if I'd didn't read so much. But then, I would never have been able to share the good news about beef.

Get Together With Your Siblings,
(You'll Be Glad !)
1995

Last week my sisters June Stockwell of Hartington and Anne Millea of Omaha, traveled with me to San Antonio, Texas, to visit our other sister, Connie Livingstone. We had a great time, laughed a lot, caught up on families, and passed out advice. My best memory is the sound of Connie and June giggling together after Anne and I had gone to bed. Seems June sat on Connie's water bed and it engulfed her.

We're sure our oldest sister, Mary Gengler, who died last year after a long illness, was with us in spirit.

Although I've been to San Antonio and visited Connie several times, the other girls had not. I could hardly wait to show them the River Walk. It is a bend of the San Antonio River that winds its way through downtown San Antonio, with shops, hotels, restaurants with out-door seating, and an outdoor amphitheater lining the river banks. It's called Paseo del Rio (River Walk). Long flat boats loaded with tourists travel the circuitous route, with entertaining boat drivers sharing historic facts.

The first time I saw it I thought it was as romantic a place as I'd ever seen. It must be nigh on to twenty years ago when I attended a meeting of the National Federation of Press Women, with my friend, Vicki Miller and other assorted Nebraskans. We sauntered along the walk drinking in the atmosphere. It was glorious.

We sat at an outdoor cafe while Vicki ecstatically ate oysters in a half shell(raw) and I ate something more civilized, and we rode on the boats with our fellow Press Women, with the smell of flowers everywhere, and Mexican music wafting about us.

We took over Dirtie Nellies, a picturesque piano bar where people eat peanuts and throw the shells on the floor, and thrilled (?) the crowd with a stirring rendition of "There Is No Place Like Nebraska," among other things.

Fast forward to July of 1995 and our arrival at the River Walk with my sisters. It was a Saturday, 100 degrees in the shade, humidity almost that high, and the River Walk was a mass of sweaty folks. We pressed bravely through the multitudes, grown people of every size, shape and attire, accompanied by a massive amount of tiny folks and all sizes in between. Long lines waited in the hot sun to ride on the boats.

My sisters did not see the romance in eating at an outdoor cafe in that heat, nor sweltering in line to get on one of the boats to ride in the hot sun over the brackish looking water.

It didn't turn out to be the romantic experience I planned it to be.

Connie, seeing my disappointment, suggested we go to Dirtie Nellies, which sits along the River Walk about a block up from where we were standing in the sweltering sun. We could have a cool drink.

We did, and even Dirty Nellie's wasn't the same. In the middle of the afternoon the peanut shells all over the floor seemed more messy than picturesque. However, it got better. The piano player was having great fun about, of all things, Nebraska! There was an entire family from Omaha at one of the tables, grandparents, parents, and grandchildren. They were in town for the Meat Packer's convention. They were having fun, and so did we.

I was hoping, however, they'd lead the group in the Nebraska Song. Maybe I thought, in a secret place in my mind, I would have to do it.

My sisters, who know even the secret places in my mind, said "Don't even think about it!"

Not to worry, I'm mature now, and behaved admirably, if I do say so myself.

Although the River Walk experience wasn't quite what I hoped, the trip was. Getting together with my sisters made me feel good all under. We love each other.

With the sure sense that time's a wastin', I advise all siblings to plan such get-togethers, the sooner the better.

Except, perhaps not on the River Walk in San Antonio in July.

Great, Great Aunt Thrice Blessed

Yesterday I stopped by the home of my nephew, V.E. Rossiter, to visit my great-niece Sheila Olson, wife of Jeff, and see first-hand what I consider a miracle, make that three miracles.

Nine months or so ago Sheila was told she was pregnant, the due date June 17. She had her baby about six weeks early, however, and then she had another one, and then another one. Triplets.

Three adorable, perfect, doll-like babies. The fact that my connection with this trio puts me in the great-great-aunt category, perhaps approaching antique, notwithstanding, I was enthralled.

All babies are fragile, but these tiny human beings seemed more so than most. They started out hovering some over three pounds, and amazingly, they are managing to look robust, in a petite way, hovering around five. They are so bitty, and so cute, it's hard not to be a complete ninny about them. A doubly great aunt has that right.

We've never even managed twins in the Rossiter family, so we were more than excited when we learned triplets were anticipated. Nobody was more excited than Grandpa V.E., who kept the sonogram handy just in case anybody wanted to look at it.

All the time she was carrying them, however, it was scary. Sheila's as big as a minute, and she had to spend much time in the hospital with doctors and nurses hovering over her. There was lots of praying going on.

But these babies are fighters. It's a good thing because they are going to have to survive their 20-month old "big" sister, Sophie's, exuberant love. Sophie likes them pretty much, but she sees no reason they can't come outside and play. Occasionally, she tries to take one with her.

Grandma Joyce claims, however, that Sophie's very good about the babies. Sophie's Mom thinks it is probably because she hasn't figured out yet that they are going to stick around. She thinks they are just visiting.

Jeff and Sheila live in Maskell, but mother and tiny people were visiting Grandma Joyce in Hartington when Shirley Stevens and I stopped by. It was fascinating because here they were, six weeks old, not even supposed to be born yet, and already they had distinct personalities, along with names that seemed bigger than they are.

Parker Jeff, a handsome little fellow, was restless, so, of course, I had to pick him up to comfort him. I explained to the little fellow that I was an expert with boys, having had five of my own. It didn't impress him. He just looked me over seriously, like a tiny judge, then wrinkled up his little face, and let out a yowl. (Judges would like to do that occasionally, don't you think?)

I was relieved to learn it was because he was hungry.

Greer Michelle, I tried to convince everybody, is the picture of her doubly great-aunt Joanie, with chubby little cheeks and cap of dark hair. They weren't so sure.

Aspen Elizabeth, who somehow found her way into Shirley's capable arms, is just as adorable as the other two, but has finer features and lighter hair than Greer. She seems shyer, too. and vaguely worried, as if she already knew about the budget deficit.

Sheila has always loved children, fortunately! Along with her husband Jeff, she'd planned to have a large family.

Only thing is, Sheila said, "We didn't plan to have them all at once." She's truly enjoying these babies, who are good little troopers. She's managing fine now, she says, because "all (?) I have to do is feed them and change them."

However, as we all watched Sophie dance around the house like a whirling dervish, and then leap off a chair into her grandma's arms, we couldn't help but wonder how she'd manage when the triplets got to be Sophie's age.

Best not to think about it!

In any case, Great-Great-Aunt Joanie will stop by once in awhile to keep you posted.

Everyone Mom Needs a
Sunny Brook Club

(Sept. '95)

Yesterday, our Sunny Brook (out-in-the-)Country Club met at my house. It is a club of neighbors who live in the area roughly south and west of Hartington, NE., and neighbors-in-spirit who did live here, but moved. They've remain in the club because of the fast friendships built over the years. One can hardly give up the Sunny Brook Club.

All my guests arrived, sometime between two and four in the afternoon, (we're nothing if not flexible) and we did what we always have done in this club. We visited.

We don't have formal lessons or programs, nor anything an outsider might see as "worthwhile." However, the women who belong to this informal little club, and others like it, would agree, the friendships we build and the lessons we learn along the way shape us in positive and life affirming ways.

Talk about your support groups! We are here for each other, literally, in sickness and in health, whether we're sweating though 4-H programs at county fairs, attending school functions, celebrating joyful occasions, or mourning our dead, we support each other in good times and bad. We cry together. We cheer each other on.

Yesterday would be an example. In our "visiting" we shared news about our families, good and bad, caught up on community news, vented frustrations, and doled out advice. We give advice freely, as one can only do with old and loving friends. It's a healthy give and take. Although sometimes it seems that we're all talking at once.

Here, as a young mother, I got recipes for my kitchen and for my life, and some solid parenting education. I'll never forget a day when we were seated around Wilma Bargstad's table and one of her kids started to bellow, and I mean bellow! She didn't move. "That's not a hurt cry," she said, calmly, "That's a mad cry. He'll be fine."

And he was. What a lesson that was to an over-anxious young smother mother like myself who jumped when her child hiccuped.

We laugh a lot at club, because we are an amusing and entertaining bunch, (she writes modestly) but yesterday, for some reason, we even got to telling jokes. Mary Fran Arens, my beloved next-farm neighbor, told the most and funniest jokes, and in the telling she gave us one more lesson about life. Mary Fran has been a grave concern for all of us as she has been undergoing a series of treatments for a cancer which we pray has been eradicated forever. That funny lady has never lost her sense of humor. She is an example of the true grit I see in all these people who are my friends. We should be uplifting her, and what's she doing? She's entertaining us.

When I joined this club some 45 years ago, it consisted of a group of older women who'd raised their families and who were, in fact, some of the founding mothers of the club, and a whole passel of us younger moms, just beginning to find our way in the complex maize of being mothers and wives. We had from six to fourteen kids per family, a multitude of boys, and we brought them to club with us. It is that kind of club. It can be quite a "thundering herd" experience for the hostess.

Now, some four decades later, **we** are the group of "older" women. The group of mothers who came along behind us, who just yesterday (it seems to me) shepherded their own thunderous herds, are tearfully sending them off to college. The only children we had at club were two tiny, well behaved girls, the last ones in each of their families.

However, not to worry, the wheel turns, the music goes on, and a younger group is beginning to show up, so there will be more thundering herds to come.

The Sunny Brook Country Club will be here for then, just as it's been here for all of us.

And someday they'll realize—just as I have—how lucky they are.

The Golden Kazoo

1996

In a very special spot on it's own little shelf, on a wall in my living room, there sits a golden Kazoo. Whenever I look at it, I smile.

We can all look back at times in our lives when something happened that changed us for the better. For me, one of those times was when I attended my first meeting of The Nebraska Press Women. It was in the early seventies. The meeting was in Omaha. I was a humble farm wife with a little column in the Cedar County News. I was "called" to the meeting by a yearning to talk to other "writers." When I got there, the thought of hobnobbing with professional journalists terrified me. I wanted more than anything to go home and tend my garden. And I didn't even have one.

The president at that time was B.J. Holcomb-Keller of Lincoln. She moderated a panel which included Ann Batchelder, then Douglas County Gazette publisher, Wilma Crumley, UNL professor of Journalism; Helen Haggie, Lincoln Journal women's page editor, and Eileen Wirth Psota, Omaha World-Herald staff writer.

I was in awe. It never occurred to me that someday they might be my friends.

Gwen Lindberg, then co-publisher of the West Point News, and Velma Price, Newman Grove Editor, the crustiest character I've ever met, took me under their wings at the meeting. I didn't know them, but they recognized terror, and wanted to help.

It took all the courage I had go to the meetings during the day. When it came time for the banquet, my courage was used up. I had a ticket, but I stayed in my room.

Pathetic, wasn't it. And yet, with that brief, yet terrifying experience, I was addicted. I wanted to be like these women when I grew up. Never mind that I was forty some years old at the time.

And grow up I did, learning more at each conference than I even knew I wanted to know. The first year I entered the contest, I did it all wrong. Eleanor Seberger, long time columnist for the North Platte Telegraph, and now a good friend, called to explain in one syllable words how it was supposed to be done. She was so encouraging that I entered again, and my column won first place in the state and then in the national contest. Eleanor was my top competition, I learned later, but she was more delighted that I was. And I was over whelmed. I was inspired. I was a WRITER.

The organization was in a transition when I joined. Organized in 1946 as "The Nebraska Women's Press Club" under the auspices of the

Nebraska Press Association, it was, with the blessing of the NPA, transforming itself into a separate organization with professional development as it's primary goal.

I wished I'd belonged when US. Senator Alice Abel (1957) spoke to the group, or Mrs. Joseph Kennedy (1960). But I was changing diapers then, big time.

I have been there, however, when Pulitzer prize winner Hazel Brannon Smith spoke, and Kathy Christenson, Managing Editor for A.B.C., a former Nebraskan, put on a workshop. I've learned from impressive people, to numerous to mention..

I've been there while we raised scholarships to worthy journalism students to $500 apiece, and built up our respected state wide high school contest .

I have taken part in workshops that taught me to be a fair (!) photographer, to "write tight," to master pesky problems on my computer, to edit, to sell ads, and taught me more about Robert's Rules of Order than anybody should ever need to know.

I'm still learning. At the Fiftieth Anniversary Convention, recently held in Grand Island, Ted Bridis, an Associated Press correspondent from Evansville, Indiana, spoke on the wonders of "Computer Assisted Reporting," and hooked me on the internet. Key note speaker Dave Tomlin, a general executive in A.P.'s Membership Department in New York, challenged me to think in broader terms about the sticky subject of small newspapers being gobbled up by syndication's. National Federation of Press Women's president Ruth Anna, a publish relations consultant from Colorado, challenged us to do something to motivate the 54 million women who didn't vote in the last election. We were challenged. Our minds stretched. What more could we ask?

Well, let me tell you. In addition to an organization that expands our professional knowledge and awards good work, we have one that inspires "personal development." I can attest to that! We cherish old members and nurture new ones, and have a camaraderie which spills over into late night gab fests and sing-alongs. We have the raucous, riotous Kazoo Khoral; dignified women, award winning women, marching exuberantly to the tunes of Sousa, playing the Nebraska National Anthem with unabashed enthusiasm, and rendering an emotional, warm and cuddly version of Auld Lang Syne. (On Kazoos!)

For years, I've directed the Kazoo Khorale. Me! The once shy, terrified farm wife. Hence the award of the Golden Kazoo from my friends! That Kazoo is symbolic.

That is why it makes me smile.

Congratulations on your Fiftieth, Nebraska Press Women. And thanks!!

It's Harvest Time in Heaven and God's Got His Man

When we're born into this game of life, the big coach in the sky issues us our mental equipment and our physical equipment, but he doesn't tell us what we're suited up for, whose team we're on, or even what game we're playing. It's up to us to find out.

Most of us, myself included, go through life trying to figure it out. That's not true of the people who the Lord has suited up to be farmers. They come out of the womb looking for a tractor. They have a special trinity relationship, the farmer, the land, and God, for they are part of His creative process. A born farmer knows how to judge the sky and how to sniff what's in the wind. He filters earth through his fingers and knows intuitively things other people can't learn in a lifetime.

Such a man was Dean Marsh. He was a farmer from the time he was a little boy, crawling down the road on his hands and knees, guiding his toy John Deere tractor with appropriate pop,pop,pop, noises, to meet his cousin Kip in the miniature farm yard they'd built in a grove.

Prophetically, Kip, the future cattle feeder, had a cattle herd with cattle made from twigs and Dean did the farming. Sometimes the two little boys moved their miniature equipment to the home of the Miller boys, Gerry and Don, to help them with their combining.

Dean's years covered the gamut in farming. He started with horse-drawn equipment and ended his days maneuvering the most sophisticated huge computer-run tractors in the business. He was never happier than when he crawled up into that cab and headed to the field. The last days of his illness, when the big tractors headed out, he'd say to his sons, Steve and Tom, "If I could just get on that tractor, I'd feel better."

Dean was a hard-driving man. His three sons, Tim (who died of leukemia at 34), Steve and Tom, were cut from the same bolt of cloth. They farm half the country. Consequently, time off was unheard of--except when Dean would trade his huge tractor in for a tiny red car and drive it in parades with his buddies from the Cornhusker Shrine. He'd say, with that unforgettable Marsh grin at full wattage, "That's what I call fun!"

Kip and I "courted" with Dean and Laura Lou, both marrying in 1947. Dean and Kip led the 4-H clubs together, we bowled together, our lives have been intertwined forever. However, knowing of Dean's suffering these past months, we were happy for his peace. Nonetheless, I lost it at the funeral watching the bravery of eight stair-step grandsons and one granddaughter, who were losing a Grandpa they adored.

The youngest, Zach, who always exchanged "pretty rocks" with his Grandpa, carefully put some in his coat pocket for this last trip.

Also, hearing the heartfelt tribute written by Steve, who said, among many other things, he hoped his dad would understand when he looked down this year and saw that the rows were not as straight as he would like them to be, because it was hard to make straight rows with tears in your eyes.

An enormous crowd attended Dean's funeral. What a tribute. The church was banked with flowers, and bulged at the seam with friends. A special tribute, one Dean would appreciate more than anybody, was the large number of farmers who were there, taking time off on a good day for field work, in a year when those days were almost nonexistent.

We lost a farmer this week. We'll miss him. Our world will miss him. But I believe the Lord has a special place for farmers, probably full of John Deere tractors and rows that need a little straightening.

He'll have the right man for the job.

Goodbye Dean. We love you.

The Perplexing Problem of No Permanent Addresses

(Spring, 1996)

As all good mothers do, I take it upon myself to compile the addresses of the entire family and send them to all our grown children. Not that any of us write letters. We are all phone people. However, they come in hand when one wants to send a birthday card or, better yet, a present.

When an address changes, I go to the permanent file in my computer called "Kids Addresses" update it, run off half a dozen copies, and send it out—again.

This is quite a job, because since the time our grown children graduated from college, they seem to move every few months. They change apartments, houses, jobs, careers, get married, or just venture out to find themselves. Just when I think they've settled down they up and move again.

However, In my wildest dreams, I never thought that one of the addresses I'd have to change would be ours. Not because we're moving. Because everybody's address is changing in our county—and all over the state. If you haven't noticed, you soon will.

It wasn't too many years ago that they added a box to our simple RR. 2. I liked RR. 2. The rural tone it set was just right. However, we had to add Box 118. It took me years to remember it, let along get used to it, because I am a math-impaired person. I can't remember telephone numbers or my social security number. I get along, however, by taking a lot of notes, and attaching numbers to big occasions, such as our wedding. Even I don't forget that.

The new address will really be a challenge. It is 56094 880 Rd. To which I must also add a zip code with four more numbers, 68739-5069. Woe is me!

I approve of the reason for the new address, which is the need for the law enforcement officials and the firemen to precisely pin point the position of anyone who dials 911 in case of emergency.

This will be possible because every road in the county is now numbered. The east west roads are designated "Roads" and the north south roads are called "Avenues." Drivers of emergency vehicles can go directly to where they are needed because they will know exactly where that place is. It's a great system.

If I were to dial 911, for instance, they would know immediately that the 560 in our address stands for the Avenue directly west of us, and the 880 Road is the road we live on. It connects us to highways 15 on the east and 81 on the west, and then it marches dutifully east and west as far as the county goes.

So whenever you run across 880 road, you know you're on the street where we live. (Ala—My Fair Lady.)

The "94" pin points us even more exactly. The nine designates the exact position of our house on that 880 road, and the four (an even number) places us on the south side. Something like that.

Fortunately, it is not necessary for any of us with the addresses to completely understand them, just so the folks who have to respond to the 911 calls understand, and they do.

Except for memorizing my address, the road numbers will be great for me because I also have no sense of direction.

A week or so ago, for instance, I was wandering in the St. Helena, Bow Valley area, and decided to head home across country to enjoy the coming of the green and the baby critters springing up all over.

I realized, suddenly, that I had no idea where I was. I went into my usual "lost" panic—until I remembered our new address.

Calmly, I drove south until I ran across 880 road. Then I headed west as fast as I could legally go, and what should appear but our house. Amazing!!

We have a year of grace with our old addresses before everybody has to update their address book. They will be a good thing. So we must look at the bright side. We mustn't complain.

The life they save may be our own.

Meet the Real Heroes of Class Reunions

(Spring, 1996)

This is the season of high school and college reunions. The season of gala gatherings of old grads celebrating, with great enthusiasm, the fact we've survived a designated number of years.

'tis the season for meeting old friends and enjoying old memories. The older we get, the more we are able to view our school years, good times and bad, with humor and understanding. We've mellowed, thank the good Lord, and therefore we've developed a deep sense of appreciation for how precious old, *OLD* friends are.

However, this column is not about graduates. It is dedicated to the unsung heroes of all these celebrations. The people who grin or grimace (as the case might be) and bear it. The folks who sit through all the hugging and kissing and telling of exaggerated stories, made much more exciting by our collective, selective memory.

These are the kindly folks who sit on the sidelines with long-suffering smiles on their faces, or gather together in protective groups to commiserate with each other. They are the ones who have put up with the honored graduates for many, years, and suffer no illusions about them—or their high school escapades.

You know who they are. They are THE SPOUSES!

The best sports in the world, they come along and go along, and even—bless their hearts—occasionally enjoy the ruckus.

Kip and I have not missed a class reunion, as a participant, or spouse. Mainly because we still live at home, and Hartington High (Kip) and Holy Trinity/Cedar Catholic (me) are right here. But, also because we each have a great fondness for our own class.

So, having been on both sides of reunion business, we each understand how the other feels

Kip graduated five years before I did, so when I attended his first reunion, I was hoping all these wonderful girls he talked about would be—well—older looking. Are you kidding? Every one of them, were the picture of health, trim, smartly dressed and beautiful. Kip was DELIGHTED to see them. They were DELIGHTED to see him.

Nobody was delighted to see me. Even Kip. They didn't even remember I existed. At least, that's what one of his old girls friends told me later. "You know," she said, "I'd have known Kip anywhere, but I sure wouldn't remember you. You don't even look familiar."

"That's because I was in the eighth grade when you graduated," I said. Well, I didn't actually say that, but I had fun thinking it. However, after I got to know Kip's class, and listened to their stories, I got hooked, and also enjoyed, vicariously, the unique bond they have.

I like to think that is the way the spouses of my classmates feel. We've had so many reunions, in fact, having just had our fiftieth, that the spouses have merged (in my mind) with our class. (Nothing they really wanted!)

Libby Goetz Dale and her husband Jack, once a football star at Wayne State, stayed with us for our reunion, as did Patty Haberer Hegert. They helped me put together a rough draft of the history of our class, which won't be finished until *ALL* the pictures and bios of anyone who was ever in our class are in. I believe this is of utmost importance for posterity. I don't know how posterity feels.

Kip likes my class too (what's not to like?) but he and Jack went home early anyway, leaving Lib, Pat and I to hang out just a mite longer.

We were motivated to stay, and stay, and stay, by a kindly (?) lady, who said, "You better enjoy your class now, because if this is your fiftieth you'll soon be dropping like flies."

Thanks (I think)so much!

Don't Worry, Be Happy
Thanks Vince!

Some years back a musical performer by the name of Bobby McFerrin introduced a song that became an overnight success. It was called, "Don't Worry, Be Happy!" The first time I heard the song it was on a tape given to me by my brother, Vince. (The late Vincent Rossiter)

It was during the height of the farm crisis, and Vince and I were both working hard trying to make a difference for our beleaguered farmers.

Vince was fighting political wars, trying to get parity for farmers, warning everybody about the impending doom and gloom.

I was fighting a psychological battle, putting on stress seminars, writing articles, visiting hurting people, trying to uplift them and cheer them up.

Vince told me he thought it was ironic that he, a relatively affluent banker, was going around preaching doom and gloom, and I, the wife of a beleaguered farmer and cattle feeder, who should be gloomy, was preaching positive thinking.

That's why he gave me the "Don't Worry, Be Happy" tape. It was his little joke. He said he thought it should be my theme song.

I am not so naive that I think we can think or sing our problems away. I've had a few dark nights of the soul. But I believe that no matter how dark the night gets the dawn will come. With that belief, and using the Lord's gifts of faith and humor, we might get knocked down, but we have the ability to pick ourselves up, and start again.

Sometimes we cause our own problems by trying to do to much and be too many things to too many people. Many folks complain about having too little time and too much to do. I complain. We all have the same problem. We can't say no.

We get so busy chopping wood that we forget to take time to sharpen our ax. We do things because we think we should, never mind if we have time or energy. Sister Marie Micheletto, noted psychotherapist, says we need to quit "shoulding" on ourselves. We cannot nurture others effectively if we don't first nurture ourselves.

Physicians, psychologists and pastors stress the importance of replenishing ourselves physically, socially and emotionally. It's not selfish. It's essential.

I read somewhere about a very generous and giving woman who was always writing checks to charities. When her account was empty, she just kept writing checks. The checks, of course, were no longer good. You can't keep writing checks if you don't have any money in your account.

Symbolically speaking, that's what we do to ourselves. If we don't take time too replenish our own physical and emotional reservoirs we will burn out. We can't keep writing checks on an empty account.

When we lay dying, we aren't going to wish we'd made more money, or had a bigger house, or served on more committees. We're going to wish we'd spent more time with people we loved. We're going to wish we'd seen more sunsets, and picked more lilacs, and danced more polkas, and eaten more ice cream.

That's why, as the song says, it IS essential to take some "Don't Worry, Be Happy!" time, just for ourselves.

It's my theme song, don't you know.

Thanks Vince!

The Controversy Over
Christmas Letters

Kip had almost all of our Christmas cards written when I got home from Denver where I'd been key noting the National Association of Teachers of Family and Consumer Sciences portion of the American Vocational Association Convention.

"But," I said to him in a whiny voice, "I didn't get a chance to write my Christmas poem." "I know!" he replied, with a self-congratulatory grin of triumph.

Kip doesn't care for my Christmas Poems. Some of you will understand.

I don't. I like Christmas letters. I like to get them, and I like to write them. Not Christmas letters from people I don't know, I hasten to add, but those from friends and relatives in whom I have a vested interest. For that brief moment in time, or half an hour, depending on the letter, I am transported into their world, and I enjoy it.

I don't even mind if they are on the braggadocios side, because it is much preferable to get the good news about people's lives than the bad. As a counselor, I encourage people to think positively, so when I get these letters in which people are celebrating the good things that happened in their lives, I think it is healthy.

I also like it when they say how much our friendship means to them, and how they'd like us to come and visit next year. And I think, for a brief euphoric minute, that maybe we'll do just that. Wouldn't they be surprised.

To you bah, humbug, scrooge types who are incensed by Christmas letters, I say bah humbug back. They take a good deal of effort and thought. I know, because of the few happy years that I wrote one.

Not satisfied with just ordinary prose, I wrote my Christmas letter in verse. Very bad verse. You know the kind. At all cost, it rhymed. I tried to be clever, of course, and I tried to be different. One year, I found it mildly amusing to concentrate on all that had gone wrong, and that year—everything had.

Since that time Kip gets the Christmas Cards into the house as early as possible, and when I am gone, he writes them. He believes the recipients are appreciative and relieved. He thinks people are so busy at Christmas they have time for nothing but the basic facts, and those are that we are still alive and capable of thinking of them at Christmas. He believes all the letters I got saying how much they appreciated my Christmas poem (two) were folks being magnanimous because the spirit of Christmas was upon them.

His take-over was shocking to me, because for years Christmas card writing was MY job. I wasn't very good at it, and I certainly wasn't punctual. I struggled for so long to get my Christmas poem just right that our cards wouldn't get sent until New Years. One year, they arrived just before Easter. Another time, desperately busy, I only got half of our list sent, so the next year, wisely, I thought, I sent the other half. This confused people who only send to people who send to them.

Our list decreased dramatically.

None of this bothered me, because I figured a Christmas card coming at any time is better than none at all, and one out of season is bound to get more attention.

This system did not work for Kip. Kip is nothing if not prompt. Prompt, prompt, prompt. He was born, as some of you also were, with an internal synchronized timing mechanism which does not tolerate even the thought of being late. He's obsessive.

Because I know this, in the spirit of compromise that has saved this marriage of opposites, I will accept his take over of the Cards. I suppose it was inevitable.

In any case, my trip to Colorado was a living Christmas card, which helps mollify my frustration about the Christmas poem. I love everything about Colorado, with the possible exception of the football team. We lived in Fort Collins as newlyweds, attending what was then Colorado Aggies on the G.I. bill.

Also, as a motivator, I got to work with a group of people who are already motivated to the max, the members of the NATFSC, which is great fun, and I got to spend time with son Bill, a mountain man if you've ever met one, and our friends Jack and Therese Thielen.

The Christmas spirit was enhanced by our arrival at our down town Denver hotel just as Denver's Christmas Light Festival Parade was taking place. Even better than that , however, was eating a meal with the Thielens, seated in their Christmas decor bedecked dining room, looking out at the snow covered mountains. I don't like climbing mountains, or even driving in them, but I LOVE looking at them.

"This is just perfect," I sighed, "I only wish that Kip could be here with us."

They echoed my wishes, and we thought of him fondly.

Not knowing that, even as we spoke, he was busily writing and sealing Christmas cards, protecting our friends from my poetry, a triumphant grin on his face.

Happy Holidays, dear readers. May God's blessings be on you all.

About Blonds and Brunettes and My Sister Connie

1995 (The Need to Laugh When Funny Things Happen)

This year, we need all the chuckles we can get, so I chuckled when I saw Marianne Beel's face on my last column. It's a rare occurrence, but once in awhile, inadvertently, it happens. It confuses some of you, I know. You may think I dyed my hair and got better looking. Or you may wonder if you ever really knew me at all.

Or you may think it's Beel's column, a logical mistake. Nobody ever looks at the authors name. One time a person I knew well raved to me about a great article she had read in the Catholic Digest. She asked me if I'd read it. I said, "I wrote it."

She didn't notice that. I understand these things. That's just the way it is.

My friend, Mary Pat Finn Hoag, Farm Editor of the Norfolk Daily News, thought the column was Beels, until the columnist started talking about her husband, Kip. Mary Pat knows both of us very well, she was pretty sure we hadn't traded husbands.

So, whoever's picture is above this column, and I suspect it will be mine, this time, just remember, I am the cattle feeder's wife and I'm brunette. The Lord's burnished me with a me a dusting of gray, but it's nothing I can't handle.

Anyway, back to Beel's face on my column. I liked it, because I've always had this dream of being a blond. They are supposed to have more fun, you know.

My sister, who was almost as brunette as I was, and is now a red head, tried dying her hair blond once. She looked marvelous. She said she also got a lot more attention, and came to the conclusion that blonds, indeed, had more fun.

That was about the time her hair started falling out. Anyone who's ever had anything dyed knows that no hair dresser will dye dark brown hair blond unless you sign a lot of waivers, so you won't sue if your hair falls out.

Connie's did, and she didn't sue. She's never been afraid to take a chance, and has a great sense of humor, so she suffered the consequences with as good a grace as possible. She said it was worth it just to be a blond for a little while, but she didn't cotton to being bald, so that's the last time she did that. .

Connie was also the first and last one in our family to get contact lenses. I don't do it because I gesture with my glasses, and don't think it would be becoming to do that with contact lenses. Connie got hers in all colors, so you never knew what color her eyes were going to be. Sometimes she used one of one color and one of the other. Connie is a little peculiar. We love her, but we never know what she'll do next.

When my Mom died she left a bunch of antiques. Mother was not so much a collector as she was an accumulator, and she had everything from silver to salts, to butter dishes, to cake plates, to goblets and a few things in between. She wasn't really attached to her antiques, she just liked buying them.

My four sisters and I divided them up. I still have mine, all in places of honor in various spots in my house. I cherish them.

Connie, however, was never much for antiques. So, she put an ad in the paper that said, "Must sell mother's antiques to fix up antique mother."

She sold them, all.

And then she had a face lift.

Mother would have enjoyed that more than anybody.

Like I said, chuckling is good for what ails us, like too much rain, too much heat, and getting too cold too early.

Thinking about Connie always makes me chuckle. I share her stories with you, because I suspect you could use a chuckle or two too. Your welcome.

Friendly Invasion of France:
The Wintz's

Fifty some years ago First Lt. Richard Wintz took part in the invasion of France as a member of an elite group, the 2nd Ranger Battalion. Lt. Wintz's men scaled the cliff's of Pointe Du Hoc on D-Day, under murderous fire, to secure the area for the troops landing on Omaha and Utah Beach. Of the 225 men that went into that battle, only 90 survived.

In August this year, France was again invaded by the Wintz family, this time a friendly invasion, as Kathy Wintz Abts and seven of her nine children retraced their father steps. They were guided in their tour by a tape their father had made prior to his death, and they are sure, as they retraced the perilous and deadly route taken by the 2nd Ranger battalion, they were accompanied by their father's spirit.

The invasion by the Wintz's was an emotional one, full of tears and laughter, something youngest son Jerry said, "We will never forget."

The seeds for this trip were planted by Verne Abts, the kindly, gentle man whom Kathy married in 1989. Kathy and Richard had planned to go to France on the 35th anniversary of D-Day in 1979, but the plan was thwarted by x-rays that disclosed a malignant spot on Dick's lungs. Dick fought valiantly, but this was a battle he would not win, and he died on February 10th, 1981

In the last days of his life, at the behest of his children, he recorded his adventures as a Ranger on tape. It was something he had never much talked much about before then. There was, of course, the on-going bantering between he and Kip Burney, a five year veteran, and a B-17 pilot in the Air Force, about whether the infantry or the Air Force had won the war. But the depth of that harrowing experience nobody really understood.

Kathy hadn't intended to go to France this year. She and Verne had gone to Europe last year on a tour lead by Dr. Brooks Ranney and his wife Vi. They knew the Ranneys were leading another tour this year, and that it would cover the battlefields of World War 11, where Dr. Ranney also served as Battalion Surgeon.

But when the anniversary of D-Day approached, and stories of it dominated the media, Kathy said "I was just a basket case." She read everything she could get her hands on, and was "glued" to the TV. On D-Day, Kathy was at home taking care of the first of the Wintz brood, six month old Sherie. She said, "I prayed all the time, and just knew he would come home, but I didn't begin to understand the danger he was in. Now I realize how naive I was."

It was Verne, whom Kathy calls "the sweetest man in the world" who suggested the trip. "Kathy," he said, "I think you need to visit France, and I think it should be something you do with your own family. You should take one of your girls with you and just go."

Two of Kathy's girls, Mary Kay (Mrs. John McCarthy of Omaha) and Marsha (Mrs. Ed Bruening of Lincoln) agreed to go immediately. "Mother should go" they said, "and we should go with her."

Then, Kathy said, "it snowballed." Five more children came on board; Sherie, (Mrs. Angelo Perry of Omaha), Sue, (Mrs. Bob Drozda of Boise, Idaho), Theresa, (Mrs. Bill Leise of Bloomington, Illinois), Tom Wintz of Los Angeles, California, and Jerry Wintz of Hartington.

Kathy's only regret was that she couldn't have had the whole family with her. Eldest son, Jim, stayed at home to take care of family mortuary, and Anne, Mrs. Larry Arens, was in the process of moving to Seward. Anne had been in France, however, with the French Foreign Study

League, so she'd had the opportunity to tour the battlefield with a map drawn by her father.

Dr. Ranney said the Wintz family made quite an addition to the tour. He and his wife, Vi, had planned the tour especially for veterans and their families. "I had the opportunity to listen to Dick's tape before we went," Dr. Ranney said, "and had an idea what they would want to see. It was actually Dick's division that successfully launched the ropes that allowed the Rangers to scale the cliffs. Other groups were shooting them off too soon."

Indeed, one of the books on the invasion has this quote. "Lt. Richard Wintz, not normally a demonstrative officer, said to his men 'you...let those charges go before I give the order and I'll put a bullet to your head'."

Dr. Ranney said another important stop on their trip was Hill 400. which was crucial to both the Nazi's and the U.S. forces, It was a "tall and narrow peak" with a view that encompassed some thirty miles. The Rangers took it and held it, thereby thwarting that part of the Battle of the Bulge. But at great cost. Of the 126 men that went up the hill, only six came down unwounded.

Dick told his family that Hill 400 was an even bloodier battle than the battle at Pointe Du Hoc. They found the hill near Bergstein, still covered with trees and rocks. It is now a national park. The Wintz family climbed to the top of a tower built on the mountain top as memorial to the Rangers, remembering the words of their father.

Kathy, dubbed," Queen Mum," by the group in England, said the family had a, "wonderful time," but that she, no longer in "complete control" had, "a few anxious moments," as her adult children, whom Dr. Ranney called "The Youngsters," shot off the busses pursuing their various interests. The girls, she said, "had a mission to shop," and, as Jerry explains it, he and Tom felt is was their duty to tour the towns at night, and maybe sample the beer. "The towns were so quiet and quaint with their cobblestone streets that it seemed almost like you were on a movie location," Jerry said.

The first nine days of their two week trip took them over the very route their father would have taken, driving down what used to be cobblestone roads and by the thick, tall shrubs that served as fences for the fields, and shields for both the Nazi's and the incoming troops.

It was a unique and rare opportunity, as Dr. Ranney, a "walking encyclopedia," provided background from his own experiences, as did the other 16 veterans on the trip. Jerry said they got a picture of the war from many viewpoints, and, "it was just great."

Even the start of the trip was symbolic, as the family traveled from England to France on a ferry that left at 11 at night and arrived at five in the morning, almost exactly the same time of night that the Rangers crossed.

"We couldn't help but think about the masses of young men who crossed this channel 50 years ago," Kathy said.

They also pictured Dick's Rangers, whom one of the veterans had called "the toughest of us all" as they climbed the vertical cliffs in the face of the raging gunfire. There hands were like leather, they were told, from their rigorous training, but the ropes were muddy and water soaked from the trans-channel trip, and it was a grueling experience. They did it, one Ranger was quoted as saying, because they had to, facing guns that had a range of more than 14 miles, and were protected by concrete bunks with walls three to six feet thick.

Their commander, Colonel James E. Rudder, said if there were men capable of knocking out this German strong point it was his Rangers.

The Wintz's also visited a museum honoring the rangers at Grandcamp-Maily. Imagine their feelings when one of the first things that greeted them was there father's name emblazoned on a memorial wall, along with all his buddies. "We'd gotten to know so many of them through the years," Kathy said. "It was quite a moment."

Another emotional moment came during the ceremony at Caen which Dr. Ranney arranged. The French Government had medallions cast on this, the fiftieth year since the D-Day invasion, to be presented to Veterans and their survivors. A French dignitary presented Kathy with the medal honoring Dick, saying,

"For your self sacrifice, for your exploits, for our freedom, I am proud to pronounce your name and to present you the Medal of Normandy."

It was quite a trip!

October 1996

This house has been in a state of suspended animation this past week. We're on red alert. When the phone rings, we freeze. Then whoever answers the phone looks at whoever doesn't answer the phone, shakes his or her head no, and life begins again.

We're expecting a baby. Not personally, of course. A grand-baby. This child will be born, perhaps before this column even hits print, to our son Chuck and his wife Kathy, daughter of Frank and Carol Cranston of Elkhorn. What could be more exciting.

Kathy chose not to know whether it would be a boy or a girl, preferring to be surprised, but Lynn Kathol of Hartington, a walking sonogram of a person if she does say so herself, took one look at her and said, "It will be a girl. Buy Pink. Count on it!" So we'll see.

Before our first Grandchild, almost perfect Kate, was born, I wasn't impressed with Grandchildren. My friends were having them all over the place, and proudly displayed pictures at every opportunity. Certainly, their grandchildren were cute, but I couldn't understand their rare ability to turn intelligent middle aged grandparents into dithering idiots. What was the big deal?

Then Kate came into our lives, and I understood. That tiny person just crept right into our hearts and there she's stayed. With a sense of awe and overwhelming love we knew, with certainty, that this little person was going to be a major player in our lives.

As all grandparents will tell you (and tell you, and tell you) watching grandchildren grow into talented, intelligent, witty, beautiful young people is a wonderful experience.

So, preparing for another assault on our hearts, we are excited.

We talked with the prospective parents last week when we journeyed to Omaha so I could have a little visit with the lovely people of St. Vincent's parish. It gave us an opportunity to see the soft ball team Chuck coaches, Millard South, play in a tournament.

It is not easy for me, a cradle Catholic, to yell for a team who's playing against teams with names that start with Saint, or Holy, or Bishop, or make some reference to Mary.

However, I've become attached to the Millard girls, for obvious reasons, and yell I did. The team did itself proud, winning the final game with "our" girls Kara and Beth hitting two spectacular home runs, while "our" pitcher, Lynnette, came through with a one hitter.

I was again impressed, as I've mentioned before in this column, by the edifying aura of good sportsmanship and camaraderie among all the teams, the coaches, the umpires and even the fans. .

What amazes me most, however, is watching the young athletes on all the teams, some of them no bigger than a minute, waggle themselves into position and with looks of utter concentration and determination on their faces, belt that ball like pros.

Of course, I'm no athlete, I <u>would </u>be amazed. At most sports I win gold as an enthusiastic bystander. In the few I participate in, winning is not a problem, it's trying to remember how much fun I'm having just playing the game.

Which brings me back to our upcoming baby production. Kathy was visiting with family members one day, musing, as prospective mothers do, about which sports this child would excel in. With a mother like

Kathy (who won a golf tournament while seven months pregnant and was still shagging foul balls at the tournament) and a father like Chuck, a born again athlete, it wasn't IF the "kid" (as Kathy calls the baby) would excel, it was in what sport.

"Excuse me," I said, "Did you remember that my genetic make up might be a factor with this child? You could be having a short brunette little girl who likes to sing and play the piano."

It would be hard to describe the horrified looks on the faces of the prospective parents.

That's probably not going to happen, because if nature doesn't do it, nurture will. The baby's drawers are full of tiny soft ball uniforms, pacifiers are soft balls, tiny sports equipment abounds in a room which has as it's theme, ostensibly, Noah's Ark.

Most of these things have come as gifts, of course, but sitting on one of the dressers is a miniature piece of equipment with a ball sitting on top of it, and a bat sitting beside it, so as soon as the "kid" stands up, batting practice can begin. Chuck bought that.

So far, there isn't a softball diamond on the living room rug—but nothing would surprise me.

Truth is, this child will be welcomed with unconditional love if it is a boy or a girl, an athlete, a musician, or whatever.

Never mind that I will be bringing a baby piano to the hospital.

Now, if you'll excuse me, I think the phone might be planning to ring.

"It's a Girl!"
October 16, 1996

A couple of interesting things happened to me since last we visited. One will make a profound difference in my life, and the other—well, it may make a difference too. More about that later.

First thing: It's a girl!! Abbie Jane Burney, nine pounds nine and a half ounces of apple cheeked delight, a cap of dark hair, long piano (!) fingers, and a sweetly placid nature. She's already sleeping four and five hours at a crack, gazing around contentedly in between, happy with her bottle and her binkie (pacifier) except when she's hungry, or her tummy hurts, and then look out. It's a rare occurrence but if Abbie ain't happy, NOBODY's going to be happy.

In fact, when Chuck called us with the news we could hardly hear him because she was bellowing at the top of her lungs. She was complaining, we think, about how hard it is for a chunky little person to be born. However, when her Mom or Dad or one of her sainted grandmothers tells her, in a soothing voice, they understand, she winds down to a series of satisfied little sniffles and a deep sigh.

I set a precedent eleven years ago by spending a week with Granddaughter Kate Johanna Burney, daughter of John and Lou Ann. So I offered to do the same for Granddaughter Abbie Jane. Specifically I offer to feed the baby at night, so the parents can get some sleep. I do this in memory of our first baby, darling Robert Keith, who visited all night and slept all day, and kept us exhausted.

Kathy and Chuck decided they'd take my offer in two parts, both coinciding with the District and State Soft Ball tournaments.

Abbie's arrival coincided fortuitously with an engagement I had to give a little talk for the AkSarBen Friendship Circle at Rolling Hills. I didn't intend to accept any talks after October 16, the day Abbie was supposed to be (and was) born. But I'd misunderstood my new friend, Carol Dvorak, thinking this one was in September. I learned of my mistake several weeks before the event, of course, but decided it could work because whatever happened I'd be in Omaha.

It was a serendipitous decision because I had a great time. Aksarben has always been a part of our lives. My sister, June, was a countess. Our boys showed calves at the Aksarben 4-H show. We loved the horse races. Such a classy and civilized way to lose money, so "My Fair Lady" ish. And the Court of Quivera has always had about it a certain mystique for me. I follow the hoopla in the paper, check out the princesses and countesses to see whom I know, and relish the pictures of the beautiful people and beautiful clothes. Quivera has been my Camelot, you see, great fun to observe from afar.

It will still be fun for me, but it has lost it's mystique—in a most delightful way. I visited with the royalty past and present over lunch, and listened to Margre Durham, mother of past Queen Sunny Lundgren, mother of immediate past Queen Jennifer Lundgren, and Carol Bell, wife of immediate past King Bob Bell tell the "other side of the story." Kings have not always felt gorgeous wearing tights under their royal robes, (In fact, newly proclaimed King Jack Baker wore a white tux) and sometimes it is literally and figuratively painful for the beautiful people to fit into their gorgeous gowns after months of sumptuous luncheons and banquets, and funny things happen.

I loved the great good humor the characters who populate our mythical Kingdom have, and understand now, how much they need it. Life is not easy for royalty, you know, even mythical royalty.

Most significant, however, was listening to Jack Baker talk about what the Knights of Aksarben are up to now, besieged as they are by the kind of events that "alter and illuminate" our times.

It's mostly good. Aksarben is not just for Omaha any more, and hasn't been for some time. It is a statewide organization and includes Western Iowa. It opens it's arms to participation on every level, and there is nothing mythical about what's being accomplished. The best of Aksarben is represented by this Friendship Circle with it's outreach to all kinds of people doing all kinds of good works.

The projects of the Friendship Circle read like a list of my favorite advocacy's, including providing funding for Community College Scholarships, supporting Youth Leadership Programs in interested communities, participating with the Knights in the Ike Friedman Community Leadership Awards as well as the Ike Friedman Awards to Students and Teachers, and providing financial assistance to the Buyers Club, Purple Ribbon 4-H Livestock Auction.

In my talk to the Friendship Circle I intended to use the birth of my new Grand baby to buy my way into their hearts if not their Kingdom. I felt it was a sure thing. Only, I got so involved with them, as we snarfed down caramel buns, worrying about whether their gowns would fit, I just forgot. Can you believe that?

So—now I suppose I'll have to join the organization like everyone else, by paying my dues.

And who knows—perhaps someday the Kingdom of Quivera will have a Page or a Countess or a Princess named Abbie Jane.

CHAPTER 4

Parenting

"Children are an inestimable blessings and a bother"

So says Mark Twain. The columns in this chapter share techniques child experts have found helpful to parents, grandparents, and teachers trying to cope with the"bother" part of child raising, so they can enjoy to the nth degree the blessing part. Included, also, are positive thoughts for dealing with the child within us as we fight our own battles as adults to become fully mature. (With me, it's win a few and lose a few!)

Love and Marriage and
the Empty Nest Syndrome

My husband, Kip, and I have six children, all of them wonderful human beings (my own assessment). We live on a farm, feed cattle, and have endured the rags to riches to rags economy that afflicts farmers and ranchers. When our children, who were born in a 12 year time span, were young we would go off to the city—sixty whole miles down the road—for just one night, maybe only once a year. Even when we couldn't possibly afford it. We'd go to dinner and take in a show. We communicated.

In retrospect, we believe those "nights out" were the most important thing we did for our relationship. Our marriage isn't perfect, or anywhere near. He's neat, I'm messy. He likes cattle and golf, I like theater and music. Nevertheless, this marriage has lasted for nearly 50 years. What better proof can I have?

It is easy to lose track of each other in the turbulence of raising a family—to wake up when the children are gone and wonder who the stranger is sitting across from you at the breakfast table. .

In the fast paced world of today, both parents often working full time outside the home, couples lose sight of the importance of making time to nourish their own relationship, which is crucial. Child experts tell parents the best thing they can do for their children is to love each other. Children should be respected and cherished, but they should understand—for their own good—that they are not the center of the marriage, let alone the center of the universe. They need to know that they are part of a working unit, and that Mom and Dad sometimes need to take time for themselves.

Not only that, Moms and Dads need to have individual personal time. Togetherness is important, but some "apartness" is necessary too. We're probably still together because of the time we spent apart, if that makes any sense. If your whole life is wrapped up in your children—or your spouse—it is not fair to either of you or to them.

I have a friend who was devastated when her youngest took off for college."I can't live without my kids," she wept, 'I am so lonely I just can't stand it. Help me!"

We talked about the importance of her finding new interests and finding out who she was apart from "mother." We pondered how silly it was for a person to sit around wallowing in self-pity when there was an exciting internal and external world just waiting for her to explore. Essentially, we decided, together, she should "get a life!"

She explored, took classes, traveled and eventually found a fulfilling part-time job. The last time I asked her about her kids she said, laughingly, "What kids?"

For years, I thought the empty nest syndrome was the figment of somebody's imagination. For one thing, when our kids left home I'd started back to college and had gotten involved in my own things. For another thing, the kids kept coming home—between colleges, between jobs, and just "between," to "find" themselves. My concerns over how I'd stand a house without children vanished before my concerns that I might never have the opportunity to find out. When the time finally came, neither we nor our children considered it so much a problem as an accomplishment.

Rest assured, I love each of our kids fiercely. They are smart and interesting and funny and fascinating to know. I want to know where they are and what they're doing. I'm just glad where they are and what they're doing isn't here. I get truly lonesome for them but—after all—what are telephones for?

If you are a Mom planning to be devastated when your kids leave, or worried about your husband becoming a stranger, or a Dad with similar concerns, I have some suggestions.

*Start developing your own interests before your children leave. It will make you a more interesting person and parent..

*Make a date with your spouse at least once a week, at the very least, once a month, even if it's just to take a walk. Do something together, just the two of you. Communicate.

Also, it's wise to be aware of and prepare for the four stages of marriage which are as follows;

*The first stage: Attraction. This is when you first realize you are crazy about each other, the "Wow and Whoopee" stage.

*The second; Attachment. When you decide to spend your life together.

*The third; Adjustment. When the white hot passion of the "falling in love" turns to glowing embers of an enduring love relationship, what psychologists call "real love." Kip and I were in this adjustment stage for about forty years. It is a time when marriages can be an emotional rollercoaster and you have to hang on for dear life. This is when marriages fall apart because glowing embers need attention to stay alive—and some people have the mistaken idea that "wow and whoopee" should last forever. (A recent article in the Time magazine gives it a maximum of four years. Ours lasted about seven hours, but that's a whole 'nother story.)It is when the blinders of infatuation give way to the realization you've both married imperfect and sometimes annoying human beings. It's work to get through this stage, but it's worth it, because it leads to the very best stage of all.

*The fourth stage. Reattachment, or more accurately, recommitment. When we finally understand what "real" love is all about. We acknowledge each other's faults, and love each other anyway. We are so comfortable we don't have to talk. If we do talk, we finish each other's sentences. It takes compromise, commitment, caring and compassion. But if you are willing to compromise, make the commitment, and treat your marriage partner with care and compassion, you'll never wonder who the stranger is sitting across the table. (Amen!)

Coping with Children, Guilt Free

I'm often asked if I think the mothers of today have it harder than the mothers of yesteryear. I would say, unequivocally, yes they do. Yes. Yes. Yes.

They have more sophisticated appliances to do their work but, some how, they have less time. They have the marvels of the TV. and computer world, but they have the problems inherent in those marvels. They must deal with a world that seems, at least to me, to be hostile towards children. They have to be constantly alert to the detrimental messages that children are inundated with in magazines, ads, on TV., in the movies, and on the street; messages that threaten their very souls. They have to be concerned, for the Lord's sake, that their child might be kidnapped.

We didn't have those problems to the extent the mothers of today do.

In addition mothers deal with more guilt than we did. We stayed at home and the guys made the living. Not better, or even happier, but we were secure in our role.

Today, Mothers who stay at home to raise their children sometimes feel that they are perceived as "less then" because they do not have "careers." Mothers who have careers sometimes feel judged as "less than" in their mother role.

At least, that's the messages I've been getting, and I get more than a few.

The guilt is unnecessary. Totally non productive. A waste of time. A mother makes her decision based on what she perceives in her head and her heart is best for her and for her family, and, therefore, ipso facto, that IS what's best for her and her family. That should be that. There is no reason here for one scintilla of guilt.

Women work outside of the home for a lot of reasons. For some it's financial necessity. For others, it's psychological, they have to work to keep from going bonkers. For many, it's a little of both.

Women stay home because, for them, it's the best decision.

In either case, they should have a strong sense of this: It is nobody's business but there own.

Whatever their decision, they need to resist the temptation to feel sorry for themselves. If you are doing something you don't really want to do, you set yourself up to be a martyr. If you've chosen to do it for any number of good reasons, remember them, and remind yourself this is what you WANT to do, as difficult at it might be. Feeling like martyr makes one sick and tired. Fatigue gets in the way of enjoying family time together, and tempers get short. It becomes a vicious circle.

It's essential, I believe, for the mother of today to evaluate her decision and do what is necessary to deal with feelings of martyrdom and guilt. For instance, whatever the mother's role, the entire family needs to contribute to doing the household chores. This is especially true for single parents. In fact, it is critical.

Children *NEED* responsibilities so they learn to contribute. Even if you can afford to pay household help, and that's not a bad idea if you can, your child need some chores. It's good for everybody, because they become part of a working unit, and develop a "we're all in this together" feeling.

A mother simply cannot be everything to everybody. However, if they allow themselves to feel guilty because they are not this mythical "super woman" children intuitively sense it, and take advantage of it.

Then parents buy children things, thinking they make up for time. Children demand bigger and more expensive "things" to make them happy. It's a bottomless pit. It doesn't work. Parents have to disabuse their children of this notion. Time is not the issue, the fact that you show you care and are interested in them is what's important.

A Missionary from India told me that the children in India were impoverished, but that challenged them to get an education and better themselves. He felt sorry for our children, he said, because they had *"the poverty of materialism."*

If children understand that it is their duty and privilege to be an integral part of a working family unit, and what they do is appreciated, they will become part of the solution not part of the problem. It takes patience, and persistence, but it works.

Suggestions to Rid Yourself of Guilt

*If you're a working Mom, review the reasons you are working, put your working role in proper perspective. Accept it and get on with life—guilt free.

*If you are a stay at home Mom and feeling house bound, arrange to do something for yourself. Take a class. Join an exercise group. Everybody will benefit.

*Don't take on roles just because others expect you to. Don't judge yourself by others standards. You've made this decision and it's just okay.

*Don't lambaste yourself for not being perfect, nobody is. Don't even try.

*Establish and stick to priorities. When you can't do everything, do what is most important and forget the rest. Unmade beds are not fatal.

*Concentrate on the positives. Understand that your children and your spouse are learning new skills and taking on responsibility, and that's good.

*Talk with your family on ways to make your work load more manageable. You may have to lower your standards and your expectations. Do it.

*Give yourself credit. Your contribution to the family is vital to it's success. You deserve your own approval.

Some Suggestions for Involving Your Family in Household Chores

*If helping you is a new thing for your family, it may (!) take some time for them to adjust. Work together on a plan. Be firm and friendly, insistent and consistent. Remember, this is for their own good. Always show appreciation.

*Put the schedule on the refrigerator and offer incentives for getting the "chores" done. Tell them, for instance, "If you choose to get your work done we can order in pizza. If you choose not to, we'll make do with left overs. It's your choice."

*Say what you mean, and mean what you say. Make sure the children know exactly what's expected of them.

I believe it is harder to raise a family today. I also know there is nothing on this earth more exciting or rewarding than having children.

(Unless it's having grandchildren.)

Dealing with Pre-Teens takes Patience and a Sense of Humor

(What Happened to My Nice Little Girl?)

This past week I got a plaintive plea from a grandparent who was disturbed because her grandchild, around junior high age, seemed to be growing away from her. "We've had such a close relationship. What can I do?"

And another from a young mother who's 13 year old child, heretofore compliant and fun to be around, had suddenly turned ornery. She had to be forced to do things with the family. "She just wants to spend all her time with her friends, or in her room, listening to that fool stereo," she said. "Whatever happened to my nice little girl?"

What can parents and grandparents do about children in this stage of development? Wait!! Wait with patience. Wait with understanding. Wait, especially, with humor. They'll be back.

These children are making the move toward independence, which is necessary for them. Their only concern, at least on the surface, is what their peers think. Studies show, however, that no matter how they act — or what they say— they are still most concerned about what their parents (and grandparents) think. It helps, although it's a mite scary, to remember how we were at that age.

Children NEED the firm guidance of parents. They need to know the rules, and what the consequences will be if the rules aren't followed. They appreciate the firm guidelines, even when they are railing against them. The message they're getting is, "my parents care enough to hang tough!" They love to tell their peers how abused they are. They need to be able to say, "I can't do that. Mom and Dad would kill me."

I had a friend who nearly had a nervous breakdown teaching junior high kids. Then she took a course on adolescent psychology, and went back into the classroom with understanding and an ability to cope. Actually turned agony into ecstasy.

Also be prepared because this is a time when children are latching on to other role models. Don't be hurt by this. Just make sure they latch on to good people. .

All of us want desperately to help the beloved young people in our lives develop self worth. Here are ten suggestions that will make that happen..

1. Spend quality time each day with your child even if it's just a few minutes. Listen, really listen, to what they are telling you. Grab the min-

utes when they happen with teens, such as when you are in a car together or working on some project.

2. Make positive statements to children as often as possible. Catch them doing things right. No one can stand a constant barrage of "no" and "don't."

3. When disagreements occur, argue only about inaccurate facts. Listen to what children have to say, but remember you will never out-argue them. *In matters of importance, parents have the right and duty to say. "You'll do this because I say so."*

4. Reach out and touch. Everyone needs it. It communicates more than words.

5. Keep laughter in your life. Laughter is the closest link between two people. Smiling begets smiling. Build family traditions that are fun. A friend had to force her teen-ager to go on their annual search for a Christmas tree. What did the little old grump do? He found the perfect tree, and even sing carols on the way home.

6. Allow children to develop responsibility. I harp on this because one (!) of my failings was being a smother mother. Don't do that!! Children need to be allowed to make their own decisions when appropriate, *except* when those decisions might be life threatening or morally destructive. Decisions about clothes and hair, for the most part, are not life threatening. Decisions about whether to drink or do drugs are.

7. Always be honest with your children. Model the behavior you want your children to copy. "Do what I say and not what I do" never has worked. Never will.

8. Separate the behavior from the child. Make sure children know it's their behavior that's unacceptable. "I always love you, but I do not approve of what you do."

9. Deal with issues here and now. Dredging up past issues blocks communication.

10. *Take time for yourselves.* Work on things that build your own self worth. Happy, well-adjusted human beings make the best kind of parents and grandparents.

What to Do When Children Get Angry

The question we've been asked to ponder in this column is as follows: *"We seem to have lost control of our children. When we try to discipline they get so angry. What can we do?"*

What I've learned through on the job training with six kids, and years of studying and teaching is this: More likely than not, children will be angry when they are disciplined, and that is okay, and even understandable, as long as they are still respectful and do what they are told to do. Kids of any age know intuitively how to poke parents hot buttons and inspire guilt, and one of their cons is to get mad so the parent will get mad back. Then, somehow, they've won. *Our job is to remain firm and friendly, and not to get mad back.* Parents they have the **right** to be respected, and the **duty** to insist on it, with little kids and grown kids. They won't be "popular," much of the time, but that usually means they are doing their job. It takes courage to stand up to kids, but when we remain firm, and they learn we mean what we say, almost miracles happen. Here is a list of suggestions that work.

1) It takes mutual respect to make a family work. Not because children are the equals of a parent, but because they have an equal right to be respected.

2) Children need encouragement like plants need water. If they are treated with positive expectations and sincere praise, good behavior and creativity flourish.

3) Children also need a balance of incentives and limits. They need to know what's expected of them, and they need to understand *up front* what the consequences are if they don't do what's expected. *Discipline needs to be swift and sure.* Children also need freedom within these reasonable limits. We want our children to know they can think anything they want as long as they behave, that they can say whatever they think, as long as their manners are good, and that they can gripe about something they have to do, as long as they do it.

4) Autocratic or permissive parents, too strict or too lenient, reap about the same amount of trouble. A lot! Children reared with few limits find it hard to set limits on themselves. Children who are stifled too much may become rebellious or angry or hostile. Or may just curl up inside themselves and be afraid. Parents who give children consistent limits, with constant reinforcement for good behavior, give them a chance to succeed in the adult world.

5) Guide your children in your own style to keep them on track, using whatever limits, expectations, incentives—and corrections—that are effective and work for you.

7) Understand that moodiness is a weapon in a child's arsenal, it is a tantrum turned inward. A child who is rarely moody may benefit from tea and sympathy. A child who is consistently sulky, surly or whiny deserves no more attention than he'd get for a tantrum: almost none at all. **Children will not do what does not work.**

8) A sassy child needs a steely eye, a raised brow, a stern jaw and a low voice that asks, "What did you say?" If a child is bold enough to continue being sassy, he deserves appropriate discipline, a time out, a loss of privileges, such watching as T.V. using the telephone or the car. (Make sure the consequence is more painful to them then to you.)

9) *Keep you sense of humor handy at all times.*

I repeat, parents have the **right** *to be respected, and the* **duty** *to insist on it. Parents who are firm are seldom popular. But inside the kids are thinking "my parents love me enough to hang tough."*

And eventually, maybe after years and years after having children of their own, your children will come to you with heartfelt thanks. It happens all the time.

PS. Remember, also, that when you change your method of parenting, children will test you, and sometimes they get worse before they get better. Hang in there, friendly, firm, and consistent. It won't be easy, but it will work, and everyone will win.

Maturity on the Golf Course????
Modeling Maturity

A week or so ago, while tootling up number two fairway on the Hartington golf course, our newly refurbished golf cart started on fire. We'd just had it fixed, and Kip told me it was fine. Except, he said, "it wants to start in high gear."

I explained that to my partner, Gert, as we shot out of the cart house. And it was fine—until the back end erupted in fire.

I share this story with humility, because it caused a lapse of maturity for me. And the subject we're discussing in this column happens to be, "How can we get our kids to act more mature."

The answer is as simple as it is complex. *The best way to teach maturity is to model it ourselves.*

Experts say, "Maturity is the ability to assume the responsibility for our own actions." It's not easy. Just when I thought I'd reached a maturity plateau, I found myself desperately trying to think of who to blame the burning cart on, before I broke the news to Kip.

Pathetic, isn't it? However, I'm heartened by an Al-Anon bulletin which defines maturity thusly: "Maturity is the growing awareness that we are neither wonderful nor worthless."

The article goes on to say, maturity has been said to be making a place between what is and what might be. It isn't a destination, it's a road." So, it isn't a plateau at all, it's an ongoing process, a road we must travel, with inevitable bumps and detours.

"Maturity is when we wake up after some staggering blow and realize, 'I'm going to live after all!'" It is finding that no matter what the blow, we have the power to work through the grief and come out stronger in the broken places. Life will not be the same, of course, but can be good again. Maturity is knowing we have the choice to make this happen.

It is the moment when we find out something we have long believed in isn't so, and parting with that old conviction, we realize we are still the same person we always were.

It is the moment we realize that good friends and family members will disappoint us, as we will disappoint them, but loved one's are worth more than a nourished grudge. So we use the powerful words, "I'm sorry", and experience the wondrous peace that comes with the healing power of forgiveness.

It is the moment we find the courage to try something we've always been afraid of. The moment we accept the fact life happens, and make the most of it. And a hundred other moments when we find out who we are.

Modeling maturity for children, therefore, is striving for maturity ourselves, realizing we'll never be perfect at it. Children learn "mistakes are for learning" by seeing us learn from our mistakes. They learn to say "I'm sorry," by hearing us say it. They learn that they will get another chance to prove themselves, because we give ourselves another chance, so we will give them one too.

When I conquered my fear of flying, traveling confidently through major airports, I knew I'd come far on my road to maturity.

But when I flew into Sioux City and my car wouldn't start, and I kicked the car, I understood I still had a ways to go.

When the golf cart burned, Kip was mature beyond belief. I should have known he would be. He always is when there's a major problem. It's when we leave a light on, or snitch his favorite pen, or his flash light, that he gets riled. Some of you may relate to that.

That's the way all of us who are neither "wonderful nor worthless" act.

The Power of Positive Affirmation

In a recent workshop, a young teacher shared this memory of her grandfather. "When I was very young, I felt I was a plain little girl, not as pretty as my four sisters. But when we visited Grandpa, that all changed. Sitting in his favorite rocker, he'd perch me on his lap, and whisper in my ear, 'You're my very special granddaughter and I love you very much.' The whisper made it clear this was to be our little secret. I can't begin to describe to you how those words buoyed me up and gave me confidence."

Then, chuckling, she told us the "rest of the story."

"They still give me confidence, in spite of what happened after Grandpa died. My sisters and I were reminiscing and I shared with them what it had meant to me to be Grandpa's favorite granddaughter. I knew they'd understand. You should have seen the looks on their faces. It turned out that Grandpa had told each of them they were his 'very special granddaughter' too."

There can be no doubt that positive messages we get as children, from parents, teachers, and grandparents, make a difference in our lives. Especially, it would seem, from Grandparents. In the workshops I present, we do an exercise which consists of trying to remember words that affected us, and Grandparents come up all the time.

Memories come slowly at first, but one person's memory sparks that of another, and soon they flow. The fact that memories of Grandparents prevail, suggests their powerful influence on the lives of their grandchildren, possibly because of their unconditional love and their ability to leave the tough love to parents. As a grandparent, I find that awesome.

Written words are as powerful, maybe more. Yellowed notes of encouragement from grade school teachers are treasured in the scrapbooks of grown men and women.

In recent weeks, the Omaha World Herald had a special section featuring poignant and inspirational memories of mothers and fathers and children that were generously shared by readers. I loved those letters. They were uplifting to those who read them, and a great opportunity for those who wrote them to express themselves in ways that will live on in scrapbooks, on refrigerators, in their minds and hearts.

The writing of letters is, in fact, a second powerful exercise we do in our classes. Parents write individual letters to each of their children, telling them something special they love about them.

It has to be sincere. Children spot insincerity immediately.

Some parents mail the letters to their children. Something about a letter coming in the mail gives it importance. Some put them under their pillows. All report positive responses. Little kids love this. Big kids are bemused, but interested. Often the letters are instrumental in opening up a stalled communication process.

A father having a hard time communicating with a teen age daughter wrote a letter telling her the things he loved about her. "You know," he said, "I'd kind of forgotten them myself."

He told us the next week that he was disappointed when she didn't respond immediately. However, he said with a grin, "That evening she was going out the door to a basketball game, and she gave me a friendly punch on the arm, a loving look I hadn't seen for a long time, and said, 'Way to go, Dad!' "

It was a beginning.

People without children often write to someone who's positively influenced their own lives, whom they'd forgotten to thank along the way. We get great response to these letters.

Some folks wrote letters to loved one's who died before they got a chance to thank them or make peace. This is cathartic and seems to begin a healing process that leads to closure.

I recommend these exercises. Encouraging words are a great gift and don't cost us a cent. It makes a person feel good, especially if we haven't communicated heretofore because of just plain laziness, or anger, or pride.

According to the author of "Children the Challenge" Dr. Rudolf Dreikers, "Children need encouragement like plants need water."

My point is, so do we all.

So say something, okay. Or write a letter. Life is just too short.

Preventing the "Birds of Sorrow"
From Making a Nest in Your Hair

Remember the old saying: "You can't prevent the birds of sorrow from flying over your head, but you can prevent them from making a nest in your hair."

Just as positive messages influence our lives positively, negative messages bring us down. There influence is insidious, because we do tend to let them nest in our hair.

It behooves us to cut that out.

We can choose to wallow in negative thoughts and let them haunt us. Or not. The key word here is "choose."

A friend once told me that she thought her career was thwarted because her father always bragged on her sister. "I've never felt I could be anything but second best," she said.

Not too long after that, her sister told me the same story about herself. Apparently their father tried to motivate his daughters by pitting them against one another. Bad idea.

Although it might be understandable, neither sister needed to allow those negative messages to continue. The only way something somebody says can bother us is if we let it. The perception "somebody bothers me," is erroneous. The truth is "I *let* somebody bother me." Realizing this gives us the power to change.

What else could the sisters do? They could do what they did. Talk it out as adults, work it through, and put it behind them. Walk in their father's shoes and try to understand why he was the way he was. Forgive their father, first intellectually, and then—with the help of God—in every other way. (Help is there. We just have to ask.)

It's not easy to let go of long-held grudges. I know. I've nourished a few. We think dark thoughts, just to intensify them.

The lump of resentment we foster is destructive to our mental and physical health. Do we want that? I don't think so. And if we use it as an excuse for failing, it is a cop out.

However, if we acknowledge those dark thoughts and bring them out in the light, we recognize their destructive force, and we can banish them. Pondering these things positively, forgiving and letting go is a win-win situation. It brings us peace.

"We cannot solve life's problems except by solving them," writes Dr. Scott Peck, author of The Road Less Traveled. This is a statement which may, he writes, impressively, be "idiotically tautological," or self-evident. And yet, "It is seemingly beyond the comprehension of much of the human race." Because everyone seems to think, "This problem was caused me by other people, or by social circumstances beyond my control, and therefore it is up to other people or society to solve this problem for me."

If we follow the political process, and how can we help it, blame is the name of the game. Meg Greenfield wrote in Newsweek, "Ninety percent of politics is deciding whom to blame." Discouraging for voters, if not repugnant, because maturity is supposed to be the ability to accept responsibility for our own actions.

They say life is like golf. It's not getting into the rough that counts. It's how we get out. Sometimes, however, we build our own roughs. We catastrophize trivialities, and lose friends by getting mad at minor events, especially when compared to the loss of a friend. We fret about things we can't control, such as the weather, or grown children. We allow negative people in our lives, ones who enjoy telling us things like, "Did you know your hair is receding," Or "Haven't you gained a little weight?" Praying for them is okay. Hanging out with them is not. They will depress us. It's their job.

If we have problems we can't handle ourselves, we need to ask for help. That is a decision that takes courage, but it saves lives. It has saved lives in our family. Maybe in yours too.

Scientific studies by eminent psychologists state, positively, that as intelligent human beings we can replace the negative thoughts we inflict upon ourselves with positive thoughts, if we choose to. Happy feelings always take precedence over negative feelings.

You don't think so? Try this simple little exercise. When you get up in the morning grumpy, grin at yourself in the mirror. The grin will become real. You won't be able to stop it. And the grumpiness will vanish. It has no choice.

In fact, grin a HUGE grin RIGHT NOW. Feel how you feel. Isn't it amazing? Then grin at someone else.

And watch as the birds of sorrow fly away.

Understanding the Characters in Our Lives

If you believe, as Shakespeare says, that "All the world's a stage, and men and women merely players," you have an understanding why we are surrounded by such a cast of characters. All lovable in their own way, strange as that may be.

For example, wisely choosing from relatives who are long gone, take my Aunt Myrtle and Uncle Charley. Please.

I loved them, but they were outrageous. My Aunt Myrtle, for instance, was something of a tattle tale. Any time she caught any of us seven Rossiter kids, or our cousins, Jim and Fran, doing anything our Dads would disapprove of (our Dad's disapproved of everything) she'd let our Dad's know. Our greatest joy as children, therefore, was to out-fox Aunt Myrtle. I've always been grateful to Aunt Myrtle because it added a certain pleasurable dimension to our lives.

And Uncle Charley was a practical joker. He didn't let being a Post Master at Walthill keep him from using the Post Office to tease his friends. Like the man who ordered a pair of pants. They'd come in four sizes too big, then two sizes too small. He finally realized his friend (?) Charley was "helping" him with his order.

My Dad also liked to kid people. During the drought years, he'd sit on the throne in the bathroom and turn the shower on full blast. Then he'd call uncle Bert. (Don't all dad's have phones in their bathrooms?) He'd say, "I'm sorry, Bert, it's raining so hard here I can hardly hear you." Then he'd happily listen to Bert groan.

I share these characters with you because the likes of them will never be again. Neither will the likes of us. We are unique one of a kind models.

Life, you see, is not a dress rehearsal. We only get one crack at being who we are, one shot on the stage, as it were. What worries me as a counselor and a teacher is those who sit in the wings, and never learn what kind of depth and breadth their character has.

What have we got to lose? Why not live life to the fullest, accepting challenges, getting more education, doing what we yearn to do. Especially, I remind myself, those of us who are—well—growing older. Time's a fleeting. Accepting challenges keeps us young.

It's good to understand too, that because we are unique and have different personalities, we will sometimes grate one other, no fault of ours, no fault of any body's. It makes it easier to get along with such people if we just understand that people have a right to be different than we prefer them to be. We have different roles. That's what makes life interesting.

A writer by the name of Gustav Ischheisen wrote the following in a book called *Appearances and Realities:*

"If people who do not understand each other, at least understand that they do not understand each other, then they understand each other better than when—not understanding each other—they do not even understand that they do not understand each other.

A good friend of ours, Father Anthony Tresnak, told about being sent to a parish which was losing an immensely popular priest. He knew his new congregation was grieving their loss. So in his first homily, he said something like this, "My dear parishioners, I know I will never be able to be Father Shane for you. But I promise you I will be the very best Father Tresnak you've ever had."

Doesn't that say it all? At best, we can only be who we are. If we accept that kindly, and give each other a break, that's all we need to do.

Understand?

The Saga of the Leid:
Having Faith in Adult Children

We came away from the Lied Center on February 10, 1996, after the "Humor from the Heartland" performance, with our jaws aching because we had laughed so hard. The Lied was sold out, and the roaring standing ovation at the end of the show rang joyfully in our ears. We basked in reflected glory.

I'd like to say, "I told you so," but I can't. The idea of daughter Juli and her comic buddy T. Marni Vos taking on a project of this magnitude had me scared silly.

Four months earlier, when Juli told us that she and Marni had rented the Lied Center to show-case their comedy routines, I was stunned. The Lied Center, for crying out loud! Where Shakespearean and Broadway plays are produced and the Russian ballet performs.

I said to her, "Couldn't you have found a nice church basement?"

Then she told me they'd hired professional cameramen to film the show (and the audience) for a T.V. special. "Your Dad has a nice video camera," I said.

Juli said, "Don't worry, Mom, whatever happens it will give us lots of material." (Comics and writers are always searching for material.)

I knew they could do it, too. Really I did. Both are experienced comics and public speakers. Juli has her Masters in Theater and Communications and directs plays, designs and builds sets, and even sews stuffed people and cars.

But not at the Lied Center.

In my defense, after my first startled reaction I never uttered another discouraging word. I just bombarded the Heavens with, probably, two rosaries a day.

My first concern was the weather. February 10. Who plans something like this in the middle of winter? When the terrible cold weather and blizzards set in back there, I may have tripled the rosaries.

Then I was concerned about getting people there. The Lied center holds some 2,200 people. Juli said they'd have to have about 1700 to break even. We don't have that many relatives. So, I prayed about that too. What else is a mother to do?

As the time came nearer it seemed the weather was going to be good, and the Thursday before the show the Lied folks told Juli they were headed for a sell out.

I began to relax. Until it hit me.

Now they had to do it! They had to perform before a standing room only crowd at the Lied. Every speaker, musician, or sportsman, knows that there are times when they are "on" and times when they aren't. They had to be "on." They had to be in the "zone." So, of course, I had to keep praying. I prayed that she and Marni would hit the ball out of the park. That they'd blow the audience away.

And they did. Just as I knew they would.

The warmth and enthusiasm of the crowd simply buoyed them up.

It's probable, off course, that the weather might have been good, the Lied sold out, and the two comics brilliant if I hadn't said a single prayer.

But then what would I have done with all that time? Go crazy???

At the end of her performance, Juli said, "Lied Center. Been there. Done that!"

What does that mean? What could she possibly be thinking of now?

I'll keep my rosary handy.

Parents and Teachers Together: A Formidable Force

(If parents don't parent, teachers can't teach!)

My Dad used to say to me "if you get disciplined in school, Joan, just plan on getting twice as much when you get home."

It was powerful motivation.

In my day, all dad's were like this. So I was appalled and amazed when I read some time back about a principal who was hit by a student, and suspended him from school. The students parents came to the school board with a lawyer and forced them, under threat of law suits, to reinstate the child.

What kind of a message was that?

I'm telling you, if parents don't parent, teachers can't teach.

That's why I said a little prayer today for all the teachers who are gathering up their books and trudging off to meet their classes. Especially new teachers, and the ones in our own family.

It's an awesome job. School boards decide on policy, the administration sets up rules and regs, but if anything is going to happen in the classroom it's because of the teacher.

So, if children are not raised with respect for authority, and are not allowed to learn from the consequences of their own actions from little on, there will be hell to pay in the classroom. No teacher should be faced with even one of those children, let along a classroom full of them.

This doesn't have a thing to do with both parents working, or single parent families. It has to do with not bringing up a child with expectations or consequences. It has to do with always picking a child up when that child falls, so they never learn to pick themselves up. A wonderful teacher in Colorado, Barb Colorosa, identified the three con's children use to manipulate. They learn them in the womb.

The first con is the whine, which we give into because it's so annoying and so easy to give into. But giving into it, we insure ourselves a lifetime of whines. If we ignore the whine, whining will cease. Children do not do what does not work.

The second con is anger. (You mean old thing. I hate you!). Children know how to push buttons, and if they can make you mad, they've won. Keeping a calm and friendly demeanor and remaining firm confuses them totally. The *remaining firm* part is essential.

The third is a tantrum in younger children, and the pout or sulk in older children. They deserve equal attention: *None!* If they can't upset you, or even make you notice, they quit. It didn't work! Children need to know what's expected of them, and what the consequences will be if they don't do what's expected. So when they misbehave, even if they protest (and they will) they know in their hearts that they had it coming. They're thinking, "My Mom or Dad (or my teacher) loved and respected me enough to hang tough."

Some parents and teachers worry about being popular with kids. Well, I have news for you. Parents or teachers who demand good behavior are seldom popular. Until, that is, those kids have kids of their own. THEN the appreciation starts.

And, don't you know, the teachers we have the most respect for and go to see later in life, are those who said "You can do better than this!" and then made us do it.

Parents and teachers working together are a formidable force.

They insure themselves and each other that later in life, *much later,* their worst problems will show up on their doorsteps and say thanks.

Flexibility

My golfing partner, Gert Konz Vonderheide, shared a story with me I thought you might enjoy. Gert spends much time at the summer home she and her husband Ben own on Lewis and Clark Lake. One memorable week, her son, Mike Konz (Managing Editor of the Kearney Hub) and his family came to visit.

The entire family planned to go to Mass in Yankton, South Dakota on Saturday night, but, as often happens at the lake, they lost track of the time and were running a little late.

Gert was to meet husband Ben at church and knew he'd worry if she was late, so to avoid that Gert took one car and headed out with the older children, hollering at them to gather up their clothes and finish dressing on the way to church. Mike and Mary Alice, followed with beauteous little Maggie.

They'd almost gotten to Yankton when 10 year old John said, "Grandma, I only have one of my shoes."

No time to turn back, of course, so Gert decided to do what any sensible grandmother would, turn John over to his father when they met outside church. He could handle it. And so she did, going on into church to join Ben. She was still a mite concerned, however, so she kept one eye on the entrance waiting for the family to appear.

It wasn't long before the Konz family came trooping happily in. Gert took one look and just started to laugh. John was limping badly. He had just one shoe on, all right, but he favored the perfectly healthy stockinged foot in such a way that not having a shoe on it would be self-explanatory. He seemed to thoroughly enjoy the experience. .

Faced with an embarrassed son, Mike came up with the limping idea. John loved it. In fact, John's friend Blake, vacationing with the Konz's, thought it was "so cool" he talked John into trading shoes (shoe?) with him after Mass.

Gert and Ben were a mite surprised when the family joined them at a restaurant, to see a different boy limping.

Mike, who doubtless has experience dealing with emergencies in his managing editor's position, turned a sad little boy's dilemma into a "cool" experience, showing both wit and wisdom.

He comes by both naturally. His Mom has wit and wisdom, besides being a good sport and a kind person, evidenced by the fact that she IS my golfing partner.

His Dad, the late John "Jack" Konz, young John's name sake, was a philosopher. He ran the Globe Clothing store on a corner of Main Street in Hartington for years, and from his unique vantage he had an overview of our small town like no other. He presided over it all with wry humor. Customers never walked in the store that he didn't have a bit of wisdom to share or a joke to tell. Also, "just the perfect thing" to show me for Kip or one of our five boys. He knew their sizes and what they liked better than I did. He was a born salesman.

His son, Dave, who now runs the Globe, is so like him it's eerie.

Jack, more than most people, understood my husband Kip, who, like his father before him, is frugal. Some might say tight. Kip and Jack had a yearly ritual. At the end of the summer season, Kip would show up early in the morning, (knowing Jack never let his first customer get away without selling him something) and get a "real buy" on some wildly colorful shirts. I'm sure Jack bought those things at market, grinning gleefully, in preparation for Kip's annual foray.

Kip wore the shirts to cattle sales. I wouldn't let him wear them anywhere else. He enjoyed them. He thought they brightened up the sale barn, and the cattle didn't seem to mind. As to what the other cattlemen thought, he didn't much care. He found out one day, however, when he overheard one tell another he could always tell where Kip Burney was sitting because he wore his pajama tops.

Did he quite wearing the shirts? Are you kidding?

Which all goes to prove, life is a lot more fun, and a lot more interesting, if we don't take ourselves or our peculiar predicaments, too seriously.

The Roses, p. 17

Hideaway Acres, p. 2

Rev. Anthony
Tresnak, p. 175

Capt. Richard
Wintz

Thrice Blessed, p. 62

The Wintz's, p. 77

The Old House, p. 11

The Dendinger Girls & Kip, p. 9

The Old Cadillac, p. 53, Yvette, Anne & Joan

It's Harvest Time in Heaven,
Laura Lou & Dean Marsh, p. 68

The Bridge Club—Back row: Don & Darlene Miller, Shirley & Gerry Stevens, Kip & Joan Burney. Front row: Clarence & Lenore Hoesing

Lori Potter, p. 16

The Honorable Mothers Sunny Welch & Me

The Entertainers Joan & Gwen Lindberg

The Golden Kazoo, p. 66—Janet Eckmann, Joani Potts, Sue Fitzgerald, Evelyn Aufdenkamp

The Graduates of '46—Lib Dale, AnneLou Weiss & Joan p. 71

The Golfers & Friends. Front row: Barb Schultze, Laura Lou Marsh, Gert Vonderheidi. Back row: Darlene Miller & Me. p. 94-108.

The Birthday Gang
Back row: Darlene Miller, Shirley Stevens, Kathy Wintz & Me. Sitting: Lenora Hoesing & Jean Carlson

The Liliac Gatherers
Shirley Stevens, Evie Litz, Lenore Hoesing

THE NEWLYWEDS

Don & Juanita Burney

Tom & Pam Burney

Kathie & Chuck Burney

My sister Connie,
the blond, p. 61 & 76
Anne, June, Mary,
Vince, Mom, Connie
& Joan

The Singles—Juli & Bill Burney

Wintering in Arizonia, p. 24

Kip and His B-17, p. 56

The Oldie Weds, Joanie & Kip, p. 182

Kate Burney, p. 80

Abraham Burney Webb

Abbie Burney, p. 82

Grandpa Kip, Abbie & Kate

The Whole Family—Back row: Tom, John, LouAnn, Chuck. Middle row: Pam, Kate, Joanie, Kathie & Abbie. Kneeling: Bill, Juli, Rob.

LouAnn & Kate & Grandma's flowers

The Burney Bunch—Standing: Bill, John, Joan, Kip, Bob, Chuck. Kneeling: Tom & Juli.

Rob & Abraham

The Swing, p. 49

CHAPTER 5

Dealing with Difficulties

Not everything that is faced
can be changed;
But nothing can be changed
until it is faced.

The Golf Cart Burneth

Mother Nature has an unwritten rule. On men's golf day, skies are sunny. On Ladies Golf Day, at least in Hartington, it's rainy, windy and cold or very, very hot!

Last Wednesday dawned rainy and cold. Except for just a hint of sun. My partner, whom I shall call Gert, and our opponents, whom I shall call Judy and Karen, were prepared. Rain hats and rain gear at the ready. Snacks and cold drinks in case of thirst and hunger. NOTHING was going to deter us from our appointed round.

Never, in our wildest imagination, would we think to bring a fire extinguisher.

It was my turn to drive the golf cart, and I did, though our golf cart had been acting up for, oh, maybe twenty or thirty years. Kip has worked hard to keep it working. This year, he's had it at the golf hospital twice. He assured me it was in A-one shape.

Except for one little thing. "Be prepared" he cautioned. It has a lot of get to it. Seems to want to start out in high gear."

I warned Gert, and she held on fast as we shot out of the golf cart house, startling everybody. "This is fun!" I said to Gert. She didn't look convinced.

By the time we started on our designated hole, #8, the sun was shining. We were ecstatic. A nice day for golf. Nothing could stop us now.

It was going up hill on hole number two that something did.

We smelled something. Smelled like hot tar. "Must be from the construction on the hill," Gert said.

"Well, I know it isn't the cart," I said, positively, "because we've just had it fixed. And fixed. And fixed."

We asked Judy and Karen if they smelled anything, or saw anything. Karen said maybe a little steam—probably from so much moisture. And Judy said, jokingly, "If it starts on fire, we'll let you know."

We decided to drive it to the top of the hill, and check it out.

We'd just started when Judy started bellowing, with that fog-horn voice honed at many sporting events, "FIRE! FIRE!! FIRE!!!" And she just kept it up.

It wasn't a joke.

Gert and I leapt off the cart with golf clubs in tow. Underneath the cart, in the back, were flames. Judy roared off in her cart, bellowing, and Gary Kuehn, the golf course superintendent, and his men, who were quite near, heard her. Actually, I think they could have heard her on main street.

Now, everyone was yelling. Gert and I were yelling too. "Get back," we yelled, "it might blow up."

Then I remembered it was electric.

Golfers, alarmed by Judy's bellowing, gathered from all over the course. By the time the fellows raced up, grabbed the long hose from the third hole, and got the fire out, we were surrounded with golf carts. Perched all over the hillside, they made me think of the cavalry riding to the rescue.

When they realized the fire was out everybody started giving me a bad time. "You'll do anything for column material," shouted a couple. "Trying to burn up the golf course!" said another. "What will Kip say?" yelled a third. That—was my first thought.

It was scary, however, especially the dramatic moment when the hose kinked and no water came out. But Gary was MOTIVATED. This wasn't just a cart burning, you see, it was a cart burning on his beautifully manicured fairway. Could be a real mess!

Well, all's well that (sort of) ends well. Gert and I just picked up our clubs and kept golfing. It was a beautiful day. Gary, a nice fellow, brought Gert's cart out to us.

Gert was relieved to be in her own cart. She surely wouldn't have wished a burned cart on me, but a few more holes of riding in mine, with those rocket-like starts, and she would probably have needed a chiropractor.

Friendships in the Garden of Life

If there are people in this world we love, but don't get to see because we are just don't get around to it, it's time we got around to it.

If we find ourselves writing Christmas cards year after year to significant others and saying, "Let's get together this year," and meaning it, but we don't do it, we need to do it.

If we've been yearning to spend time with family members, or army buddies, or school friends, or anyone who's had a positive impact on our lives, we need to pick up the phone. Make a date.

Have I put this strongly enough?

Gather up your siblings or your friends and hug a little before it is too late.

We think we have all the time in the world. We think our siblings and friends will live for ever. They won't. Mine didn't.

We can't live our lives always afraid that people we love are going to up and die. We should, however, understand it's a possibility.

When that happens, we need to be able say, "I'm so glad we spent time together last summer."

Years ago, one January morning, Kip said to me, "I've got a hunch we should fly out to Mesa and see Dad." So we did. Kip's Dad was to celebrate his 95 birthday on January 15. We were planning one whing-dilly of a celebration, but it was to be in Nebraska in the Spring. We had compiled a guest list of his many friends. I was working on the program, under the vigilant eye of Dad's second wife Grace.

Then Kip got this sudden notion we should spend his actual birthday with him, and we did. We had a great time.

Dad didn't make it till spring. See what I mean?

Big deal, you might say, he was 95. This past month, my friends, a niece and a nephew of ours (54 and 49 respectively) had heart attacks. They are doing fine, but it fills one with a sense of urgency. You see, we can't always wait until Spring.

I'm not trying to depress anyone, just to encourage all of us to slow down long enough to do a little hugging with our cactus friends. It's a stress relieving activity, good for our hearts, and for all the rest of us.

Who are cactus friends? I will explain.

It's my theory that the people in our lives resemble flowers. There are the friends who are like African Violets. They take a lot of tending, and won't hang around if you don't do things just their way. Some people are good with African Violets and think they are worth the trouble. I am not.

Next come the philodendron-like friends who need some care, but are still there for us even if we neglect them a little. We love them for their loyalty and their stamina, so we make sure to give them the care they need. An occasional card or letter, a phone call, a lunch along the way, and philodendrons flourish and add much beauty to our lives. They are good friends.

The very best, however, are the cactus friends. We may not see them for years, but our friendship never changes. They uplift our spirits and gentle our hearts. They are GOOD for us, and we are good for them.

Often they are relatives, who neglect us as much as we do them, but are always there for us if we need them, as we are for them. Sometimes they are friends from the past with whom we've experienced life in a special way, thus forming an unbreakable bond.

A cactus friend can also be a new friend, one we know instinctively is worth making an old friend out of. Rare occurrence, but it happens.

Cactus friends are all soul mates. Friends who love us in spite of ourselves.

If we are very lucky, these friends live near us, even in our house.

Often, however, life has taken us down different roads. We get busy, and they get busy, and we don't get to see them anymore, much as we'd like to. Much as we NEED to.

So let's think about someone we love, dear readers, who we haven't seen for a long time. Someone who makes us smile just to think about. And whatever time of year it is, let's make a resolutions to find that person and give him or her a hug.

It's heart healthy!!!

Learning to Have Fun
Just Playing the Game

A man I know well, we'll call him Jim, had the terrible habit of losing his temper when he played golf. He vented rage on his fellow golfers, sure that they had sneezed, or talked, or taken a breath in his back swing. He yelled at people who talked too loud in the next fairway, swore at passing cars, planes flying overhead, and even loud birds. And his poor clubs! They landed in lakes, up trees, around trees, and broken over his knees. And that was just on the first hole.

No amount of friendly counseling by his peers had any affect on him. He began to find it hard to find a foursome to play with.

Now understand, when not on the golf course he was witty, urbane, and mostly calm. So when he left town to seek his fortune elsewhere, the folks who didn't golf with him missed him.

His golf buddies breathed a sigh of relief.

He came back to visit, and Kip, one of his golfing buddies, wasn't looking forward to playing with him. I knew how bad it was when he told one of the boys, "I'd rather golf with Mom."

He called Kip when he arrived, saying "I can't wait to get out on that course." Kip joined him, reluctantly.

He came back in a state of shock.

"He didn't get mad. He didn't throw one club. He didn't swear. We're all wondering if he's not ill."

When Jim arrived for supper, I asked him about his unusual behavior. He laughed, and said. "One day I flew into such a rage that I threw my whole golf bag in the lake. That even embarrassed me."

"We were playing in a tournament, and the fellow with me was so disgusted he told me off. I said, "I'm sorry, but I get like that when I'm not golfing as good as I think I should.""

He said, "You know Jim, you'd be a lot better off if you'd admit to yourself you're not as good a golfer as you think you are, and just be satisfied with the kind of golf you're capable of playing."

"It was a watershed moment for me," Jim said. "I saw the light. When I accepted the fact I wasn't as good a golfer as I thought I should be, the pressure was off. Now, I just enjoy the game."

Human beings are peculiar. We take up a sport to have fun, and then ruin our fun by thinking we're better than we are. .

I have a good friend who has had her ups and downs ever since I can remember. But she only remembers her downs. When she's in one, there's no convincing her "ups" are on the way.. No matter how many good shots she has, you know what she remembers? The bad one.

"You'll get better," I say, "You always do."

She wants to hit me along side the head with her pitching wedge. She can't stand me spouting positive thinking. Most people can't. To bad for them! I say it because I am right! I did a whole paper on this subject. (I knew you'd be impressed.)

In my research I learned that sports psychologists say we don't lose our ability, we lose our mental acuity. Our concentration. We undermine ourselves with negative thoughts. We over think. When we relax and start thinking positive thoughts, we get better. Trouble is we get obsessed with parts of our game, and forget to just get up and hit the ball. Even professional golfers have slumps—on national TV. Think of that!

The sad thing is, to quote a favorite adage of mine, that we spend so much time concentrating on winning, we forget how much fun we are having just playing the game.

Not that we can't get better if we put our minds to it. Quoting sports psychologists again, sports are learned skills. Although we may never be champions, if we learn the basics, use positive mental imagery to go over them, and practice, practice, practice, we WILL improve.

But if we keep making the same old mistakes, and blaming them on somebody else, nothing will change. We get so busy chopping wood, that we forget to sharpen our ax. (Adage #2.)

I was my own guinea pig while doing this research. I worked on bowling, my game of choice. My average has always been around 115/120 (Not good, but we had fun!) Research stressed that I was bad because I thought I was bad. If I changed my thoughts, I'd improve. Could this be? So, I did. I learned the basics, something I'd never bothered with, visualized myself bowling 200 (not likely!) and practiced. Raised my average some 50 points and once in awhile I'd get in the zone and bowl a 200 game.

It worked! Nobody was more surprised than I was

Thus it is with life. Sometimes, success is just as far away as our own heads. We simply have to change our attitude. But, as in sports, as I said, we get so busy chopping wood we forget to sharpen our ax, and we concentrate so much on winning, we forget how much fun we're having playing the game.

The point of all this is we need to cut that out!

Do I hear an "Amen!"

Just Call 911

Sometimes I'm envious of people who just refuse to get involved, sticking their heads in the sand like ostriches , not realizing how much they've left exposed. Unfortunately, or fortunately, as the case might be, I can't do that. I came from a family of advocates who fight for what they believe in, no matter what the cost.

I was under some stress about a cause I was involved in this past week, when a friend of mine, Roberta Hoesing, called me to give me encouragement. She knew, she said, how hard I'd been praying to do the right thing when she read an editorial that I'd written in the paper taking a tough stand on a controversial issue. She assured me, since I had put it in the hands of the Lord, I could be sure I was on the right track.

I told her how tough it was to know, and how, in this particular case, I'd implored the Holy Spirit for help. Then one night at one o'clock in the morning, I sat up, wide awake, and I knew, without a shadow of a doubt, that I should write what I wrote. I was sure it was an inspiration from the Holy Spirit, working through my sub- conscious, and I went with it. All the way. Typing until nearly four in the morning.

Still, I told Roberta, when I got up in the morning, and read over what I'd written, a tiny shadow of a doubt crept in. What if this inspiration was just something I ate?

She assured me again that I was on the right track, but, she said, "That's why I called. I thought maybe you could use the Lord's 911 number.

"Could I ever!" I replied. "What is it?"

She says, "That's it. Nine, one, one."

"Say, what?"

She said, "It's the ninety first psalm, first verse: 911. Get it? Actually, the whole ninety first psalm is what you need."

Upon hanging up, I headed straight for my bible and found the Lord's 911 number. Oh, my, how it spoke to me.

Biblical scholar I'm not. Those of you who are, are already way ahead of me.

It is the psalm that starts with,"

"He who dwells in the secret place of the Most High shall abide under the shadow of the Almighty. / I will say of the Lord, "He is my refuge and my fortress. My God, in him I will trust." /Surely he will deliver you from the snare of the fowler and from the perilous pestilence./ He shall cover you with His feathers, and under His wings you shall take refuge; His truth shall be your shield and buckler./ You shall not be afraid of the terror by night, nor of the arrow that flies by day.

It goes on, of course, including that most comforting psalm, "For He shall give His angels charge over you, to keep you in all your ways."

So, was I still worried?

Well, a little.

But was I vastly comforted.

You bet!

Thanks, Roberta.

The Agonies and Ecstasies of Golf

The wonderful thing about golf is that no matter how bad you feel about the way your life is going, no matter how worried you are about things in the outside world, you can go to the golf course and feel worse.

You go back, because you make par on just one hole, or just one long putt. One day, you may par the course, and you are raised to the mountain top.

That's what I hear, anyway. I'm waiting for that day.

I'm a great believer in the power of positive thinking. I use it in bowling, and it works. I have not used it too successfully with golf, although I know it can be done. Golf is a head game, after you get the basics down. I'm still working on the basics.

Unfortunately, unlike other things in life, in golf it is possible to try too hard.

Take the Saturday, July 1995, when we had the member guest tournament here on our beautiful little course in Hartington. We'd ask our son Chuck, and his bride of one year, Kathy, to be our partners. Chuck's handicap is 11 for 18 holes, and Kathy's is almost that. I do well to golf in the high 50's (on nine holes).

The men had a terrible first day to golf, 100 plus heat, with almost that much humidity. That proves you don't have to be crazy to play golf, but it helps.

The women golfers (and I enjoy saying that about myself) had a perfect morning, with a little sprinkle of rain that felt good. Kathy was in rare form. She can hit a ball over 200 yards, and she did. She drove our cart, hit the ball, and then I would hit the ball, and hit the ball, and hit the ball, until we finally got to where her ball was.

So I tried harder. And I got worse. It all culminated with me getting in the sand trap on our last hole and taking four strokes to get out.

Kathy golfed a 43, and won the tournament, and the longest drive, and the longest putt contest. I won a contest also. The shortest drive. Striving for a positive thought, I settled on the fact that I'd gotten more exercise than Kathy. (31 more strokes)

It was a nice day, though, I'd had one exceptional putt. One out of 74. So, you know I'd be back....the next Wednesday , as a matter of fact.

That was Women's Day, and I was golfing with my partner Gert Vonderheide. Our opponents were Barb Hochstein and Bette Merkle. These girls are GOOD golfers, and hit the ball a country mile. But we don't mind playing them, even with an ever- looming sense of impending defeat, because they are fun. They play bingo, bango, bongo, with a vengeance. I love bingo (first on), bango (closest to the pin), and bongo (first in the hole), because no matter how bad you are playing, you have a chance to win something at this game.

Kip will never play it. It ruins his concentration, and the first time you measure the length of a putt with the flag pole, the golfers following you get really steamed.

Well, Gert and I were playing pretty good, as were our opponents, when we came to the hole where I'd had the misfortune to get in the sand trap I whined about above, the one I almost never got out of. So I had to whine again, telling the story to Gert and Barb and Bette in vivid detail.

Gert and I plumped our balls on the green to capture bingo and bango, and Barb hit hers in the sand trap. So did Bette. A feeling of guilt came over me. Certainly my talking about my trouble in the sand trap hadn't put that in their heads. Had it?

It got worse. There's a terrible lip on that sand trap, and Barb hit the ball three times, unsuccessfully. So, feeling guilty as I did, I suggested she come out the end. She did. The ball came right out. And went into the other sand trap.

It only took Bette three to get out.

The upshot of all this is that Gert and I won our match, and also, on the last stroke of the last hole, we won bingo, bango, bongo, for the cool drink of our choice.

Although I did feel guilty because of whining about the sand trap just before our opponents spent a weekend in it, I still felt good about winning, which is, as you know, better than losing.

However, the looming sense of impending doom descended on us again when Barb and Bette said, "we'll see you next year" with an ominous tone in their voices.

They didn't really care about the game, I knew that, but they really get ticked off when they lose at Bingo, Bango, Bongo.

Getting Rolled Over by Sherman Tanks

I had a call the other day from someone from afar whom you do NOT know, who was having trouble with a really "mean" person at her place of work. She felt angry, demeaned, and—worst of all—scared. She was letting this person run over the top of her and didn't know what to do about it. She was even considering giving up her job.

Now, understand, this wasn't her boss. It was just someone working with her.

Do nothing drastic, I said, let's think this over. I did some research for her, and—since we all deal with folks like this occasionally—I thought you might be interested. This kind of a person is called a "Sherman Tank," by Robert M. Bramson, Ph.D., in his book, "Coping with Difficult People." Another term is "Hostile-Aggressive." They combine active aggressiveness with hostility in a fearsome way.

They come out charging, not always physically, but their whole demeanor expresses, "Attack." The very fierceness of their demeanor robs their victims of the ability to even think, let alone respond coolly and competently.

To understand the behavior of Sherman Tanks we need to understand that they truly believe they are always right, so when someone disagrees with them they quickly become outraged. They overwhelm people, and sometimes achieve their objectives, but at great cost, because of the negative feelings they create.

To cope with Sherman Tanks, according to Dr. Bramson, we need to stand up to them. If Sherman Tanks think we are weak they will continue to roll right over us.

However, we should not respond with fear and rage. It's a no win situation to have an open confrontation with a Sherman Tank. They thrive on open confrontations. Let them run down, and then stand up to them calmly and state whatever you need to state. Get their attention, carefully, and ask them to hear you out.

If we resort to Sherman Tank's tactics to respond to them we are perceived to be one too, and nobody wins. If we simply speak our point of view in an assertive, friendly and non-combative manner we turn confrontations into a discussions. Sherman Tanks hate discussions, and sometimes they get worse before they get better. That's because they are very good at fighting, they've perfected their skills, and they cannot believe it when their tactics don't work. This is how they get their way.

The point is not to defeat the Sherman Tank, because we might win the battle, but not the war. Sherman Tanks tend to seethe and then they plot to get even. We are simply trying to help them realize their is a more civilized way of doing business, and—in any case—we are serving them notice that we will no longer be overwhelmed by their tactics.

Nobody, even Sherman Tanks, will continue to do what does not work.

It takes courage to deal with a Sherman Tank in this way, but it's more satisfactory than being run over by a bully.

The amazing thing is, according to Dr. Bramson, when people with this type of personality find they cannot overwhelm you, they begin to treat you with respect and may even make friendly overtures.

It's not easy to be friendly, because when the Sherman Tank has been abusive you want to react with anger, and get back at them. Big mistake, as that is a lose- lose, situation, and may get in the way of developing a mutually valuable relationship, which would be a win-win situation.

As annoying as Sherman Tanks are when they are rolling over us, we a have a whole different attitude when they are on our side.

Interesting isn't it?

You Want to Look Like Susan Sommers?
Here's how......

The things you don't learn in a Doctor's office. Kip and I were in Omaha, waiting for a routine check up with Dr. Palmer, the man who's led the partially successful attack on Kip's rheumatoid arthritis. Scrounging around for reading material I came across a Cosmopolitan, a magazine I would probably only read in a Doctor's office, and opened it up to an article by Susan Sommers, whose advice I wouldn't ordinarily seek.

The title of an article caught my attention. It was, "Getting your diet back on track."

It turned out to be an article I need to refer to on a weekly basis. Because, you see, even people such as myself, who are most weight conscious, people who KNOW how to eat right because they've been through dozens of weight loss programs, even people highly motivated to keep weight under control because they have to zip up their clothes occasionally, even these people sometimes (often!) lose control. I know. I am one of them.

So I picked up some hints which I thought might be helpful to me. Since misery loves company, I'm sharing this slightly edited and augmented version with you.

*Fast for a day to condition your body and to crave less food. Focus on liquids only—fruit and vegetable juice and lots of water.

*Don't eat anything between meals

*Don't skip breakfast. In fact, have your largest meal in the morning to better burn off the calories.

*Increase exercise at least twenty minutes a session, something about speeding up metabolism to burn off more fat.

*Eat slowly. Savor your food. Slow down your mouth muscles. It takes at least twenty minutes for your tummy to tell your head you're full.

*Keep low calorie snacks on hand, carrot sticks, apples, etc.

*Never eat standing up. (This is more effective than it sounds.)

*Use visual imagery, SEE yourself slimmer, visualize your body getting rid of the weight. See yourself in your skinny clothes. Positive mental imagery in weight loss (or sports) is a powerful ally.

*Leave a little food on the plate. (Almost impossible for people who have been raised to clean their plates because of the starving children of Armenia.)

*Write down what you eat for a week. (Shock therapy!)

*Before you ever sit down for a meal, decide what you will and will not eat. (This really works, especially for banquets, brunches, or buffets.)

There it is. Good luck and happy, healthy eating to us all.

Hope we see less of each other in the future!

Warning Signals on the Dashboard of Life

Staving Off Strokes

July, 1992

My family tends to pop off with strokes—or, in the case of my Mom, live for five years, bedfast. Considering my family history it behooves me to take a serious look at what causes strokes. Perhaps it behooves you too. Let us look together.

The following information comes from the Stroke Foundation, no less. I've read it several times, but even more carefully after a fainting spell, after which I was given a thorough physical. My Doctor said, "I have good news and bad news." Said I, "let me have it." Said he, "The good news is that we can't find anything wrong with you. The bad news is that you fainted, and there had to be some reason, so you better think about it and slow down."

I try to, because I am truly afraid of having a stroke. I don't know if I could be as courageous as the stroke survivors I've met at the motivational workshops I've conducted, let alone their valiant caretakers. They listened kindly to my words, but I felt inadequate. They were the teachers.

A stroke is an injury caused by a blockage of the blood flow to part of the brain. Over 500,000 Americans have a stroke every year. It's the third most common cause of death by disease and the leading disabler of adult Americans. A stroke can happen to anyone at any age, but incidence does increase with age.

You and your loved ones can help prevent a stroke if you exert some control over the risk factors in your lives, and become aware of the factors over which you have no control. Listen up while I name a few, and decide if these warnings are significant in your life, or that of someone you love.

Causes of stroke......

1) Smoking. (I've never smoked. I feel for those who can't quit. I say, get help and DO IT. Easy for me to say!)

2) Excessive weight. (I am a food-oholic. I will always have to watch what I eat.)

3) Abuse of Alcohol. (A social drink occasionally doesn't hurt, but if you feel even mildly guilty about your drinking, it is time to think about it.)

4) Use of cocaine and some amphetamines

5) High Blood Pressure (Mine runs about 90 over 60, no problem here)

6) Cholesterol (With diet and exercise I am down to 204, Alleluia!)

7) Polycythemia (abnormally thick blood).

8) Presence of diabetes mellitus.

9) Oral Contraceptives. (Cause of Iris Doolittle's stroke at 28.)

10) Stressful daily life conditions. (Guilty, guilty, guilty.)

11) Sedentary life style. (Not enough exercise?)

12.) Family History of stroke or heart disease. (Oh yes!)

It's estimated that over half of the people who have a stroke have previously experienced a Transient Ischemic Accident (TIA). A TIA is a blockage of blood flow in the arteries of the brain. TIA's are temporary, but if any of the following should happen, contact your doctor immediately. As our own Doctor Charles J. Vlach says, these can be *the warning signals on the dashboard of life.*

A) Sudden severe headache.

B) Blurred or double vision, or partial or complete loss of vision.

C) Numbness, weakness or paralysis of the hand, arm, face or leg.

D) Difficulty with swallowing

E) Dizziness, fainting, loss of balance or sudden falls.

F) A recent change in personality or mental ability, including sudden memory loss or forgetfulness.

E) Loss of speech, or difficulty with reading or understanding speech.

The good news is that there are many things to be done now for stroke victims. There's drug therapy to inhibit clotting in the bloodstream if the stroke victim gets to the doctor or the hospital as soon as possible. There are also great places for stroke survivors to go for rehabilitation.

If these things had been available when Mom had her stroke, the outcome could have been significantly different. What a great thing it would be if this knowledge had been available.

What we should be concentrating on now, however, is how to *prevent* strokes in ourselves and those we love. And how fortunate we are that these educational tools and medical options are available to us.

The Best Intentions

The afternoon was a disaster. I had the best of intentions, but everything went awry. Have you ever had afternoons like that?

I've been working on book #3 for the last year or so, trying to wrestle columns around in my computer, and having a miserable time. I finally realized I had to run them all out and pile them up where I could SEE them. Now I'm working enthusiastically

It was about time. My deadline was last week.

I swore I would not leave my computer until I was finished, and was working diligently, eyes bugging, back aching, little zings of carpal tunnel visiting my wrists, when the phone rang.

It was Shirley Bogue. She was having Wednesday Afternoon Club in her lovely abode in Hideaway Acres, could I come? Ordinarily, I'd be delighted, but I had to say no. I was working.

Shirley doesn't suffer "no" willingly. "Betty Moser is coming." She said, "Don't you want to see her?" Of course I did! "And you need a break!" How did she know? I always need a break.

Okay, I'd come, but I'd drive myself and leave early.

"No problem," Shirley said.

Little did we know.

Rain fell in a deluge Wednesday, so the gravel road short cut to Shirley's was out. As long as I had to drive through town anyway, I decided, I take some of the "girls." Jean Carlson was also driving, and she called to relate Shirley's message, "Park in the lower driveway, you won't get so wet." The lower driveway is precariously carved into a hill. The last time I parked I got stuck in a snow bank.

However, I always do what Shirley says. (Used to, anyway.) So I parked in the lower driveway pulling in next to the cars already there, but some of my riders couldn't get out. So I backed out, always affable and eager to please, and turned off the car, prepared to have a lovely afternoon of bridge. It never occurred to me to worry that when I backed out my car blocked the other cars in the driveway.

Not until later. Our car lights turn themselves on and off, but they were doing it erratically on the drive up, so I'd turned them on.

Well——the battery was almost dead when we got back to the car, and after I'd tried to start it forty times, it was. All the cars were parked facing the same direction, so using cables was not an option.

I wanted to call a tow truck, but Hideaway folks being what they are, dependent upon one another, Shirley insisted she called Dana Wall. Like a knight in shining rain coat Dana came, rain sluicing down his face. He hooked my car to his jeep, not an easy task, and pulled it backwards, me steering, Bob Bogue shouting orders. That made it possible to go nose to nose with Bogue's car, which was parked on the hill where I should have been parked. We got it started.

But it had taken a long time and the seven women I was holding up had much better things to do with their time then wait around. Although they were trying very hard to be good sports.

I was the person who was most mad at me. With the best of intentions I blew off an afternoon of work, kept seven friends captive in the Bogue driveway, caused Shirley and Bob and Dana to get thoroughly soaked, and worried the heck out of Kip, who was trying to call me on a "locked" car phone.

And that isn't all!! I had lousy cards, and Betty Moser didn't even come.

CHAPTER 6

Dear Joanie:

You have to
believe the buds
will blow, believe in
the grass in the days
of snow: Ah, that's the
reason a bird can sing
on his darkest day
he believes in
spring.

(author unknown.)

About Believing in Spring

"Almost all of us from time to time seek to avoid—in ways that can be quite subtle—the pain of assuming responsibility for our own problems." (Scott Peck.)

During the farm crisis years, after I'd gleaned a number of degrees and certificates indicating I was officially educated as a Psychological Counselor, Bob Bishop, then editor of the Nebraska Farmer, asked me to write an advice column for the Nebraska Farmer and Colorado Rancher/Farmer. A column such as this, he said, would be a valuable service to the readers, and help ease pain along the way. How could I not accept such a request?

Especially since I knew I'd be able to back up any knowledge and experience I had with a multitude of available experts.

I also knew, from studying those same experts, that a counselor's aim is not to solve another person's problems , it is to help them figure out ways to solve it themself. Or not. It's their choice.

We've tackled a multitude of subjects, including the merits of gasohol and of gambling, and ways to cope with adultery, ungrateful children and workoholic or unappreciative spouses. Readers share heart-breaking stories, and funny ones, and offer their own wise words on various subjects. Controversial subjects bring in thought-provoking letters and irate letters. It's a great experience, and continually adds to my own learning process.

The columns in this chapter are those that have been requested again and again by readers. They tell me these columns have enabled them to transcend some of their difficulties. That is music to a Counselor's ear. Perhaps, they will help you do a little transcending too.

The Power of Saying Please
and Thank You

When children are young, most parents stress the importance of saying "please" and "thank you." At our house we called these "the magic words." When a child would forget, simply saying "And what are the magic words?" would bring the desired response. If they really wanted something, it would be, "Pleeeeeeeease!

These magic words never loose their power. I thought about this as I pondered the question I'd been asked to write about. It went something like this, *"I never hear any words of appreciation. My spouse says I should just KNOW I'm appreciated. My boss says he'll let me know when I'm doing something wrong. I feel that I really need to hear that I'm doing something right once in awhile. Am I wrong?"*

No and thank you for asking. I appreciate it.

Spouses, or bosses, or anyone else for that matter, would benefit greatly if they just realized how important it was to show a little appreciation. People work harder, more creatively and are happier when they're appreciated, and so is everybody around them. If more people expressed appreciation, oftener, this world would be a much happier place.

I will illustrate, altering the stories to protect the innocent.

My first example is of an employee who started a new job with enthusiasm, lots of fresh ideas, and a ton of energy. He made a difference and he knew it.

The problem is, he never got one word of appreciation. Not only that, the more he did, the more he was asked to do. Seldom was there a "please" before a request, and NEVER was there a thank you. The crowning insult was that after putting in many extra hours on a successful project, he had to fight to get paid.

While adults are self-motivating to a point, we still need appreciation and encouragement much like plants need water. If we don't get it, even the strongest of us are apt to dry up and wither on our vines.

That's what this employee has done, in effect. He still does his job, adequately, but just what is required. No enthusiasm. No fresh ideas. No energy.

The other side to this coin is the importance of showing appreciation to our employers. An employer spoke to me about the many things he'd done things for his employees in his work place. No matter what he did, however, they never seemed to appreciate it. They just come up with more demands. Frustrated, he's darned if he's going to do anything else.

You see the problem, don't you. By not showing appreciation, by not saying appropriate "please" and "thank you's" for good work, these people are fulfilling an old axiom. They're "cutting off their nose to spite their face."

It happens in families as well as work places. If you reinforce good behavior, it will continue and it will grow.

Positive reinforcement, when deserved and sincerely given, changes the atmosphere of a work place, or of a home, or of a committee, or any group of people who work together.

Catching people doing things good, instead of pouncing on them for mistakes, accomplishes near miracles. The attitude "mistakes are for learning" encourages the ability to learn by trying. Studies show that people who work in a positive atmosphere are infinitely more effective, more creative, happier in their jobs, and less likely to change jobs. The rewards to the employer are manifold.

Employers also respond to this kind of positive feedback.

Let's go over it one more time. Not showing appreciation, never saying please or thank you, creates a negative atmosphere. Showing appreciation, simply being nice to people, creates a positive atmosphere and is good for business. Positive reinforcement creates a "we're all in this together" feeling, which is infinitely more fun than the alternative.

Try it, you will really, really like it. Please!

No matter how old we are or how young we are, how rich or how poor, whether we run a corporation, or push a broom around our kitchen, we will *always* appreciate the magic words.

Thank you!

Farmwives Vent about
Lack of Appreciation

This will be painful for some folks to read. Especially those who need to read it. The response to the column on saying "please and thank you," was overwhelming. Here are excerpts from some of those letters, altered to protect the innocent.

First letter. "I have been a farm wife for many years, and I've driven cranky trucks, loaded bales, done field work, hitched up machinery, run augers, climbed bins, hand sprayed weeds and inside bins, run for parts, toted meals, worked cows, fed steers, chopped thistles, checked fences, both electric and non, summers and winters, sick and well and pregnant, and with small children in tow....Pleases? Thank yous?? No! But lots of yelling, name calling, criticism, temper tantrums, threats if I failed to jump high enough when he gave me orders to; and demands for my time, attention, strength or thinking when I had none left to give..."

Another letter, "Farming I like, but it's getting to be more than I can chew. The guys around here are workaholics, in love with our cows. They do nothing but work and are always tired and testy. Nobody gets any enjoyment out of life. I help outside too. My husband has heath problems, works all the time, and appreciates nobody. The boys are just like him. A little appreciation would go a long way around here."

And one more, "Since my husband died I have been the GO-fer for the sons and sons-in-laws who work our farm. Whatever I have planned, it's expected that I just hop to. I'm fed up. I love them, but sometimes I don't like them much. I KNOW I'm needed, but I feel used, and I would almost kill for one word of appreciation. "

The writer of the first letter went on to give valuable advice. In order to survive, she said, she got counseling and took a job off the farm. She wrote, "I am stronger, more open, and a happier person as a woman with an outside job, where people have more manners, and I get more pleases, thank yous and RESPECT than I ever had as a farm wife."

That's an option, and a good one. The Harry Truman axiom, which could be taken literally in the case of farm wives, is "If you can't stand the heat, get out of the kitchen."

Many of the women who wrote, however, were willing to stick by their men, though they sometimes act like insensitive clods. They just wanted ideas about how to survive. One farmwife asked, "Can you write something for folks like me who have problems like mine, to keep me sane and happy?"

It's tough to be in a position where you're belittled, unappreciated, and verbally abused. It's not hard to advise what one should do in the case of physical abuse. Get counseling, get help, and if that fails, get out, fast, and don't look back.

But psychological abuse is another thing. Some men were raised in this kind of abusive atmosphere, and don't know how to act any other way. This is the way their Dad treated their mother. We need to help them change.

They won't change, however, unless the women in their lives get "more than they can chew," and demand to be treated differently. We have that right, you know.

This is darned near impossible for a woman who's never spoken up. Often these women love farming as much as the men in their lives, and even love their men, though they "don't like them very well."

Doubtless there is fear involved. But nothing can be worse, in cases like this, than doing nothing. Wives and mothers may not be able to change their men directly, but if they change themselves, their men will have to change in response to them.

It is wise to get counseling, as our first writer did. Church social services provide counseling for little or no cost. In lieu of that, talking with a pastor or a trusted friend will help you start the process of change. This is a subject that needed to be aired. Congratulations on having the courage to write. You're on your way.

We'll discuss this more in upcoming columns.

Such vitriolic vituperation is
not really necessary
(Jimmy Durante)
The Other Side of the Story

After the letters on difficult men, it's time to hear the other side of the story. See what you think...

This reader, who prefers to remain anonymous, writes as follows: "I share your concern about the health and happiness of farm families. I feel that your column omitted one ingredient of the gender equation. It is my impression from witnessing at least three generations of spousal controversy, there is a common thread that continues from generation to generation. I base my observations from being in the homes of family, friends, playmates and employers over the past 60 odd years."

The common thread is obvious, he says, and this is it: "Women are much more vocal in expressing their emotions than men. It's my opinion that the feminine version of a message carries a lot more descriptive embellishment than that of the male counterpart. As Jimmy Durante would have said, 'such vitriolic vituperation is not really necessary.'"

"Many of my male counterparts share my philosophy. To complain is a woman's prerogative. It goes with the territory. We listen to the harangue and try to sort out the real message. In most cases the criticism is justly deserved, but it always hurts. Sometime a little. Sometimes a lot. Whether it is grandfather, father, son or grandson, we are still perplexed why the message can't be delivered in a calm civil tone."

"I admit there are farm husbands who are absolute ingrates. My feeling is they are an extreme minority. There *are*, however, a plethora of husbands who do not express appreciation. To me the key word you used is sensitivity. Men in general do not feel a need to be praised for being maxed out in all their efforts. That women feel differently, in many cases, doesn't even enter their minds."

"There are and have been exceptions, but for the most part family farm life has been and still is a harsh, harsh, life. Much more so than it is popularly portrayed. One person's label of workaholism might be another's devotion to a mutual goal in life. We need to realize in our expectations of successful farm life together that there is going to be a lot of stress along the way. We need to realize that husbands and wives do not emotionally respond to that stress in the same way. They haven't for generations past, and to me, its doubtful if they ever will. However, if we can't understand the other gender's behavior we can strive to understand how they feel and moderate our behavior accordingly."

The writer goes on to say, "My comments to you on this subject are not intended to be judgmental of either husbands or wives but rather thoughtful observations of what I have observed over the years. While it is true that both of us know tragic examples of ill-behavior, there are many couples who have successfully coped with life's difficult challenges. There is hope!"

I could not have written this better.. The "hope" in my mind is the raising awareness of the need to try to understand each other. Life would be a lot more pleasant if we did. Many people accept a life of grimness and bitterness just because they fail to communicate their needs to each other.

It is possible to learn. It could make a big difference. That's powerful motivation.

Upward and onward!!

Coping With Difficult People

This column, as promised, will share some proven ways of coping with the difficult people in our lives.

There is a good book that's been around for awhile called "Coping with Difficult People," by Dr. Robert M. Bramson, Ph.D. Although Dr. Branson primarily writes about people in the work place, his descriptions also fit folks who sit at our kitchen table on occasion. As we go over his seven categories of difficult people, someone may pop up in our minds for every category. It may even be the person who looks back at us in the mirror every morning. Here they are:

*The Hostile Aggressive, who bullies by bombarding, making cutting remarks, or throwing a tantrum.

*The Complainer, who gripes incessantly but never gets any closer to solving the problem.

*The Silent Unresponsive, who responds to any question with a yes, a no, or a grunt—or not at all.

*The Super-Agreeable, who is always reasonable, sincere, and supportive to your face but never delivers a promise, never follows through.

*The Negativist, who responds to any proposal with an "It won't work."

*The Know-It-All, who wants you to recognize that he knows everything there is to know about anything worth knowing.

*The Indecisive, who stalls any major decision until it's made for him and refuses to let go of anything until it's perfect—which means never.

Our goal in dealing with the difficult people is to do so in a way that will not accelerate our problem, but will diffuse it. Following are some coping strategies:

1) Assess the situation. Try to understand where difficult people are coming from. Not to excuse their behavior, but to better understand it. Walk a mile in his (or her) shoes. Also we must assess own behavior honestly. Listen to the tone of our voice. Do we explode back, whine, sink into silence, or just sit and suffer? You see the point here don't you? How much a part of the problem is our own attitude?

2) Stop wishing the difficult person were different. It is not possible to change a person by wishing. However, by doing something to change ourselves, by changing our own attitude or way of responding, we change the dynamics, and difficult people will have to change to deal with us.

3) Get some distance between yourself and the difficult behavior. If not physically, psychologically. For farm wives this means take some time for yourself. This is a crucial step and takes courage, but if you really want to affect a change, it is necessary. We need to do what many have done before us, get an outside job, volunteer for a life-enhancing position, go to a counselor, join a group, sign up for a class, read self-help books, do SOMETHING! Broaden your horizons and your thinking. Build your own self worth. It IS possible to bloom where you are planted. If you can't, transplanting may be in order.

4) Formulate a coping plan. The coping plan can be as bold as standing up to the Difficult Person and People in your life and saying, "I will no longer put up with this kind of behavior. It is not acceptable and I deserve better." Not in an accusatory tone, more in a "I'm sure when you realize how destructive your behavior is, you will want to change for the sake of our relationship" tone.

Difficult people back down when they are stood up to, especially when it is done firmly, but with love and respect. Give them a specific list of changes you want them to work on. Such as, "When you speak to me in a denigrating tone, I will leave the room (or the house)and not return until you speak to me with respect." Or "This is the time I'm serving supper. After that hour, it will be in the oven and you can help yourself." Of, "I want you to smile at me at least once in the morning." (This is more powerful than you might ever think.)

Hope this helps. Good luck!!

Difficult People: Review

Let's review. In the past few columns we have been sharing thoughts on the difficult people in our lives. The September and October columns extolled the virtues of treating people positively, saying please and thank you. In the November issue, we heard from farm wives who never heard a positive word from their husband or their family and they were hurting. In December, we tried to throw some light on the kinds of negative people we have to deal with in this world, and begin discussing ways we could do that. We digressed in January, to present a very well written "other side of the story" which explained why men have trouble dealing with women.

We've established some facts. 1) There are difficult people in this world. We work for them, or with them. Often they are relatives. Sometimes, we marry them. 2) People have a right to be different than we prefer them to be, but they do not have the right to make us miserable. 3) However, sometimes they do. Perfection is not a human attribute. They will disappoint us, and we will disappoint them. What can we do?

Understanding human nature helps. We all have different personalities. Folks will grate on our nerves, no fault of ours, no fault of theirs, because we are fundamentally different types of people. I am a clutterer, and my husband, Kip, is neat. Very neat. We've been married for 47 years. There isn't a day, I'm sure, that my clutter doesn't annoy him. I try, but sometimes I fail. He loves me anyway. So, about twenty-five years into our marriage, he gave up. He built a divider in the middle of our office so he wouldn't have to look at my desk. It's called compromise. It works.

If we just understand that we will never understand some people, and try to appreciate them for their good qualities, it helps us put up with what annoys us.

It is futile to try to change someone, especially if their annoying traits are inborn. The only thing we can change is our own attitude. In doing that, we change the dynamics of the relationship, and it WILL be better. Try it, you'll like it. I promise!

In a truly hurtful relationship, we need to get distance between us and the hurtful person, if not physically, psychologically. If it's a relationship we can't give up, we MUST plan to nurture ourselves. *People can not hurt us unless we let them.*

It helps, also, if we understand that for the most part men and women operate on different frequencies. Men are less verbal than women. They a have a shorter attention span. They aren't interested in what my husband calls "psycho-babble."

For instance, if your husband asks if you had a nice day, and you say "Fine!" in a tone that tells him it was anything but, he just hears the "Fine!" and goes about his business. Woman interpret and analyze while men just ignore. The message we give is not the message they receive. Often, they don't have a clue.

We're hurt. They don't understand. When women nag, men just tune them out. They get hurt, but they'd never admit it. So the problems just compound themselves.

That's sad, because the greatest healer in any relationship is heartfelt communication. That can and will happen if we sit down *when things are calm* and say, "When you act like this, or say that (or whatever) it really hurts. Can we talk? "

In one of the letters we received a wife was in great pain because when she and her husband went to a dance he never danced with her, just flirted with other women. Whether it's husband or wife, that kind of behavior really hurts! And if it is never addressed, never confronted, it will never get any better.

The three essential things necessary to building a positive relationship are simple. They are: 1) Communicate, 2) Communicate, 3) Communicate.

If we need a mediator to start communication, so be it. And if we haven't communicated on a feeling level for years, we're probably going to need one. Find someone you respect, preferably a pastor, or a counselor, or a good, neutral friend.

If you are in a hurtful, destructive relationship, please do *something* to change it. Don't just sit and suffer. It eats up your insides. No one needs that!

Every journey starts with a single step.

Take that step!

Communication Troubles

(1995)

The letter was hand written, and very short. *"Dear Joanie: A couple of years ago it seemed as if we had the world by the tail. Now everything that can go wrong is going wrong. Last year we doubled up on our hog operation, and you know what happened. This year we decided to raise calves, and we lost a lot of them to the spring storms. Now we're worrying about even getting our crops in the ground. But the worst thing is, we're hardly speaking to each other, just when I think we really need to talk. It's not like this was anybody's fault. What can we do?" Signed, "Hurting."*

Dear Hurting; Your letter will ring a bell with anyone who's ever been in this wondrous business of agriculture. We love it, but we sure have to learn to live with peaks and valleys. And, of course we need to talk. Lack of communication only causes more stress. Talking things out eases the tension, promotes understanding, and where problems are concerned, starts the healing process. It is the best stress reliever available to us.

However, just saying "let's talk!" sometimes meets with resistance. What works best is to take advantage of times to talk that just happen. For instance:

*Use time in the car when you're running errands or traveling some place.

*Use time when you're working together, or playing together, whether you're fixing fences or doing dishes, or golfing, or fishing, or whatever. Something about having your hands busy lets your mouth move more easily.

*Get things started by sharing your own feelings. "I'm really concerned right now, I'm afraid of how things going. Are you afraid too? Can we talk about it?"

*Make a practice of sitting down with a cup of coffee at a special time every day, maybe after a meal, and talk about how things are going, how each of you are doing. Kip and I talk every morning over breakfast. Sometimes we don't say anything of much importance, but we talk.

*Listen for openings when it seems your spouse is ready to share feelings. Don't deny those feelings, or say he or she shouldn't worry, or try to make things rosier, just listen and try to understand. Every time you share, just a little, it's easier.

Sharing feelings will also help us make decisions we need to make. And maybe they will be tough ones, like getting a second job, giving up farming, changing jobs, moving, whatever. Many people have had to face the reality that farming can't be just a "way of life" it also has to be a profitable business. So it's up to us, with the help of our financial advisers, to figure out if what we're doing is ever going to work.

If it isn't, we have to bite the bullet and make some changes. Communication is essential during any change process. It is essential, between spouses, between partners, and within families.

While the decisions we have to make are painful, they are also exciting. We are taking charge of our lives and facing a new beginning. I've interviewed many a farm family who left the farm reluctantly, crying all the way. They are doing just fine, and wonder why they didn't leave sooner.

Even if things aren't that bad, when tough times come on the farm, we need to communicate. Working together, it is much easier to pick ourselves up, dust ourselves off, and start all over again. Communicating our feelings, in good times or in bad, is not only beneficial, it is critical to our mental and our physical health.

Another important aspect of this; if someone is hurting, and wants to talk things out and work out what he or she should do, we just need to listen. They don't need advice, right now, nor somebody to tell them what they did wrong. They just need someone who cares, who will give them the greatest gift we have, listening.

So, dear Hurting, this might work. Let your spouse read this column, and then give him some space and some time, and he will talk. Deep down inside, he knows he needs to. Good luck and God bless. Let me know how things go.

There's Nothing Funny About Adultery

The letter touched me, and because an open discussion of this problem might be helpful, I will share excerpts, and some of lengthy epistle I wrote in response.

Edited for reasons of privacy, the gist of the letter was as follows; "You always talk about the importance of humor, but how can a person laugh when their life has been devastated by their husband having an affair. There's nothing humorous about adultery. My husband says it's me he loves, but I just can't forgive him. What can a person do to survive a hurt like this? Tell me, have you *never* had times in your life when just couldn't find anything to laugh about?"

Believe me, I've had times. I have had my dark nights of the soul. I've done my share of grieving. Therefore, I can personally vouch for the truth of what follows.

Whenever we have a loss, whether it's a loved one, or faith in a loved one, or a job, or the use of a limb, or any loss at all, it is a terrible psychological wound, and we have to heal, just as we heal from a physical wound. Healing means we have to let ourselves feel the pain of the grief, work through the denial, anger and depression, cry our tears, and make our way, on a roller coaster of emotions, to acceptance. This is the way things are. I can't change them. So what can I do to help me get on with life.

We cannot choose what happens to us, but we can choose how we respond. As the old axiom says, "We can't keep the birds of sorrow from flying over our heads, but we sure don't have to let them make a nest in our hair."

When we get to acceptance, sometimes a long and painful journey, we come to understand that although life will never be the same again, it can be good. We can make the best of it, or the worst of it. It's our choice. We can, with a little help from the Lord, forgive when we are wronged. There is a great healing power in the generous gift of forgiveness, which lifts up the forgiver as much as the forgivee.

(I'm talking about forgiving a person for whom an affair is out of character, not the philanderer who makes a habit of it. That is a whole 'nother epistle.)

Sounding off to me, the obvious anger, is a good sign the healing process is underway. It is important, also, to get counseling. There are hurts we simply cannot handle alone. Also, to try to understand how this adultery thing happens, and that it just might not be the end of the world. Men and women think so differently. Sometimes, men are just damned fools, but then so are women. For the most part, people who get involved are grasping at youth, risking everything they really value for a mess of potage, so to speak. Love, it isn't. It is, for most, temporary insanity. And they will look back at it with disbelief. That knowledge may not come instantaneously, but it will come. Imperfect human beings, which we all are, sometimes goof up, big time. Look at what fools some of our esteemed political figures have made of themselves, along with a host of religious figures, taking a chance on giving up everything they've worked for a momentary fling. Inconceivable! But it happens.

Time, which truly heals all things if you let it, will also gradually heal this. Faith can be rebuilt. It seems impossible, especially when you are in the throes of anger and grief, but what happens is you come out with more understanding about the pitiful weakness of humanity, and understanding this, and forgiving it, you will be stronger in the broken places.

It takes great courage to let go of something like this, to quit scratching the scab off the psychological wound and making your own self miserable, but you don't want to be mad all of your life. It helps to ask the question the esteemed advice columnists always advise, would you be better off without him? Probably not.

It also helps us to forgive others if we remember a time when we did something stupid and badly needed and wanted forgiveness.

Humor can be a help at a time like this. Not in depths of grief, perhaps, but as the healing starts. Laughter gives a brief respite from emotional distress, and is a great help to mental and therefore physical health.

And someday, years and years down the road, you will look back at this mountain and hardly be able to see it, for the mole hill it has become.

Can a Person Work Too Much?

You bet!!

A letter from a farm wife, signed "Lonely" told of being married to a man who was a workaholic. She wrote,"Everything is work, work, work, work. All we talk about is work. All we do is work. If I suggest we take a weekend off for fun, he looks at me as if I'd suggested robbing the bank. Can a person work too much?"

Yes!!! Studies by eminent psychologists offer proof positive *that taking time off raises productivity* and avoids burn out. It's good for us, and good for our business. Many folks in agribusiness, male and female, don't understand how crucial this is.

There was a time when Kip spent every waking hour working with cattle or at cattle sales or talking to cattlemen. Our vacation? A Livestock Feeder's Convention, what else? If I planned a trip, I had to make sure we didn't miss his favorite cattle sales on Tuesdays and Thursdays and Fridays. Some trip! Sound familiar?

So, as many wives of workaholics do, I learned to do my own thing. I went back to school, and the rest is history. This arrangement can work, sort of, and is better than sitting at home brooding. Some of my friends, married to workaholics in other occupations, also do there own thing. It's adopting a "don't worry, be happy," attitude.

It's not easy, however, and in our case, events happened that changed our lives. Two of Kip's older brothers, Wid, 63, and Dr. Dwight Jr., 64, died. It was a terrible shock, because we thought Burney men lived forever. Kip's dad died at 95. His Grandpa died at 86, and his 92 year old brother came from Phoenix for the funeral.

Deciding life might be shorter than he planned, Kip glanced around, noticed I was still there, and decided we should start doing things together. What a shock—for both of us. It took some adjusting. But we have BOTH learned to enjoy it. Truly!

The point is, it's best not to wait for a tragedy to realize time is a precious—and limited—commodity. I take an old clipping out when I get so busy chopping wood that I'm forgetting to sharpen my ax. It's an eye opener. The question asked is this:

"Are you running your life, or is it running you?"

*When did you last spend a day or an evening doing something completely frivolous, totally non-productive. Has it been longer than two months? Take heed.

*Have you ever spent an evening with friends or attended an affair you've been looking forward to—and found that you are too tired to enjoy it? If so, look closely at your priorities. You are doing too many things and making some bum choices.

*Have you been telling yourself you should get a complete physical check up (including eyes and teeth) but you've been too busy? If you've been putting this off for more than a year, you are not being fair to yourself or to *those who love you.*

*Do you keep running into people you genuinely enjoy, and have been meaning to see, but just can't get around to it? If so, you're cheating yourself. Sit down and schedule time for them; dinner, luncheon, or just getting together for a cup of coffee. Even if you have to schedule it three months away. *You'll be so glad you did.*

*Can you honestly say you are calm, in control of your life, fulfilled, pleased with yourself, secure in the knowledge that you are making more good decisions than bad ones? If you can, congratulations!

If you can't, read these questions one more time.

I know I will.

More About Thank You's

Nothing teaches a lessons like shared personal experience, so I am grateful to Oscar Uldrickson of Wausa, for a letter in support of my column about the importance of positive reinforcement, as in saying "please" and "thank you."

Oscar wrote about his experiences in the Navy in W.W. 2, saying, "The military is a harsh place, with harsh words and chew outs. Now that works with some and not with others. There was this certain fellow who had been chewed out until he was so beat he just couldn't do anything. So they transferred him into my division. I sorta knew how he was feeling, and so I said to him 'There is a water fountain that is not working right. Would you check out some tools and see what you can do with it?'"

"After awhile, I went to check and found the fountain working just real well for a change. So I looked him up and told him the truth—that he had done a real good job on the fountain."

"From then on he became a very dependable worker. I just got off his back!"

"Those other fellows looked at him in amazement and asked me "what did you do to change that man."

"Just a few kind words!!"

Oscar went on to say that he carried that philosophy into civilian life and if he hired help and one of the wasn't doing their best, he'd put him on something he knew he could do real well and then complement him on it, and "the first thing I knew, he'd been doing everything well."

At the end of the day, or the end of a job, Oscar writes, he would give them their pay, and then, he writes, "I would pay them what money couldn't buy, I'd tell them how much I appreciated them helping me!"

"Sometimes" Oscar writes, "just a few kind words are the best medicine!"

Thanks, Oscar, I couldn't have said it better.

Dealing With Depression

I usually don't respond to anonymous letters, but this one had a question in it which has, at some time or other, been of concern to all of us. If not for ourselves, for someone close to us. It was, "Sometimes I get so depressed life doesn't seem worth living. Can you help me cope with my blue moods?"

Depression is a feeling we all have to deal with occasionally. It is the common cold of our daily existence. If we sense it goes deeper than this, we need to try to understand why we feel the way we do. We can do that by talking about our feelings to someone we trust. Problems stuffed inside fester and make us ill.. Problems shared become challenges to be solved. Talking—with a good friend, or a pastor, or a counselor—relieves the tension and helps us put things in perspective.

Sometimes, however, we don't know exactly why we're feeling down. It's as if we have an itch we just can't scratch. Again, talking about our feelings is a good way to get a handle on them, and to ferret out problems that won't surface.

Feelings—depression, anger, envy, joy, love, whatever they are—are normal. We have almost every range of feelings, at a greater or lessor degree, every day of our life. Denying them does not make them go away. Admitting them, and dealing with them positively, puts them in perspective.

We need to pay attention to how we feel, listen to how we sound when we're talking to others, feel the tenseness and weariness in our body. It seems so simple, but often we don't want to acknowledge how we feel, so we pretend the feelings aren't there. It's human nature. Denying them, however, won't make them go away. Neither will taking our frustration out on others. If we are yelling at everybody and finding fault everywhere, it's time to go home and look in the mirror.

We can choose to wallow in misery if we want to. We can go through life blaming everybody for our problems. We'll be much better off, however, if we can take responsibility for ourselves, look at what is happening in our lives, accept what we need to accept because there's nothing we can do about it anyway, (like growing older and kids leaving home), or change what we are able to change.

Sometimes it will just be a matter of changing our attitude about ourselves or about others. First we have to accept ourselves. We are who we are, with our own unique physical and psychological equipment. We aren't going to be opera stars if we were born monotones. We won't be sports heroes if our talent is playing the piano.. See what I mean? Once we truly accept that, we can get on with being the best we can be with some degree of enthusiasm. Accepting ourselves, we will find it much easier to understand and accept others.

People have a right to be different than we prefer them to be. It's ironic how often we pray for somebody else to change, never getting the message from on high that the person who needs to change is the person who's doing the praying.

The good news is we CAN change. Human beings can raise their spirits by conscious endeavor. We can bring ourselves out of the doldrums by learning how to nurture ourselves. That means not bottling up problems but talking them out with someone we trust. It means eating healthy, exercising, doing things that we enjoy, and **choosing** to think positively.

It means breaking overwhelming tasks into do-able segments, setting reasonable goals, and working toward them enthusiastically. Just the decision to do SOMETHING will dissipate the mental haze of depression.

However, and this is very important, there is such a thing as clinical depression which is a serious illness and calls for medical and psychological intervention. If you have the slightest suspicion that you, or anyone you love, has sunk into that kind of deep depression, you need to get help immediately. IMMEDIATELY!! Please.

Midlife Crisis

I'm writing this column in response to a phone call asking "Can you write something to help us with our Dad?" Seems Dad was model father and a good husband, until he hit his late fifties. Then he begin to dress inappropriately, started openly flirting (if not more) with other women, neglected his work and his wife, and took off on occasion with no explanation to anyone.

Mom, who spent her life as a housewife and a home maker, waiting on this man hand and foot, willingly and with enthusiasm, was stunned and humiliated.

But she is no wimp, this lady. She got fed up. Packed the man's stuff, and told him to get help or move out. Only problem is she had a fatal flaw—she loved the man.

So, although he did move out, he found that having no one to take care of him was not wonderful, and talked Mom into letting him come home. Surely, Mom thought, (remember the fatal flaw) he's seen the error of his ways, he will change.

He hadn't, and he didn't. He just reestablished himself at home, and continued his bizarre behavior. "What can we do to help?" asked my caller, "It's tearing the whole family apart."

Some men go through a mid-life crisis which starts with the gradual realization that they are getting older. Their hair starts getting gray, their tummy bulges, and the beautiful young woman they married has the nerve to get older too. She doesn't "excite" them any more. They get scared.

While most men deal with these feeling rationally, some literally panic. They go into denial, and pursue youth in a way that might be described as temporary insanity. They change their life style, pursue women, tromp on their wives feelings and try to ignore grown kids (a visible sign of aging.) In other words, they act like damn fools.

They aren't fooling anybody, and in the long run, they don't even fool themselves. Somewhere along the line, if they are lucky, they wake up and realize the goal they are pursuing—endless youth—is not attainable. They begin to appreciate the benefits of growing older with someone comfortable who has the same memories.

Sometimes these men need a wake up call. Their acting out may be the sign of deep depression. They need counseling. Will they get it on their own? Probably not. The have an addiction—to youth—as powerful as an addiction to alcohol or gambling, and as in other addictions, they are heavily into denial.

It may be necessary, with the help of a counselor or pastor, to have an intervention, a gathering of family members and friends who will sit down with this person and in a loving way tell him how his unseemly behavior is affecting those who love him. It's a painful process, but it is effective, and a jump start out of denial.

As important as helping your father, however, is helping your mother. This kind of behavior by any spouse is a drastic blow to self esteem. Counseling is essential. By learning how to nurture herself, and filling her time with life-affirming activities, she will start, painfully and slowly, but surely, to finding her own potential. She will need to work through her own depression and grief, cry her tears, and deal with her anger, but if she truly works at it she WILL heal. She will get to the stage of acceptance. She'll find she doesn't need her husband or anyone else to be a whole person.

You think that won't get his attention?!

If she allows him to use her while he's indulging in his self- destructive behavior, however, she's enabling him to continue. All the nagging in the world by her (or the family) isn't going to change him, because he's obviously decided it's the price he has to pay to maintain his status quo, so he'll ignore it.

But if she regains her self respect, he will have to change in response to the changes in her. She may even decide he's not worth the trouble, and dump him. It's happened.

Except for that fatal flaw, that business of loving him. So, she'll probably take him back on more equal terms—hers.

If he's very, very lucky!

Years ago, a friend of ours was gloating about his freedom because his wife of many years was gone for the week. Then he said, "You know, I miss the old gal. We sit together in the evenings and don't say a word, but I miss having somebody not to talk to."

Building that kind of comfortable "old slipper" long-term relationship is hard work, but it's worth it. It may not be glamorous, or even exciting, but it's soul-satisfying, and heart healthy.

Show this column to your Dad. A man who has caring children like you, and a loving wife like your Mom, is a lucky man. He's bound to be smart enough not to throw that all away.

Good luck. Let me know what happens.

To Bet or Not to Bet
Musing About Gambling

1995

Last year, about this time, the subject of gambling came up in this column. It's come up again. Gambling has become a big time money raiser in most of the mid-western states, with all kinds of factions out after people's hard-earned money.

I shared some of the comments in response to that column then, but didn't get to all of them, because other subjects came up and had to be attended to. The question, "So, what do you think of gambling after it's been around for awhile?" sent me to the files to find a letter from an erudite lawyer in Fremont which makes all the sense in the world.

Excerpts from the letter. "First, I do not oppose gambling if it involves some participation by the gambler. This is present in poker, bridge, blackjack, dice, horse races, athletic events, and a host of other events...the participant, if reasonably intelligent, should not expect to lose more than 10% of the money wagered."

The percentage of loss in other forms of gambling is "tremendous," he writes. He considers government-authorized lotteries a travesty, saying "Our legislators, at a much earlier time, recognized the evils of lotteries and made any participation or promotion a crime," but those laws have been changed because of "easy money envisioned by politicians and bureaucrats."

"Lotteries impose a harsh tax because they are supported principally by those least able to afford it." He talks of people spending time gambling "mindlessly" when every community has "an almost desperate need for more adults" to be involved in activities with children, etc.

When the federal statue prohibiting gambling was amended to exempt state-approved lotteries, "Pandora's box" was opened. States adopted lotteries, and then other states HAD to adopt them to protect themselves. (Or so they thought, anyway) The same thing happened with cities; passing laws to permit gambling to keep the resources from going to other cities.

Our writer suggests, and I concur, that our politicians should enact some "truth-in-gambling" legislation, to let people who do participate in the various types of gambling offered know the odds, "the almost certainty of losing" and understand that what is loss is not paid "by the government or the operator, but by themselves and their friends and neighbors who participate in this non-activity?"

What can be done? "Only a mass lobbying effort by some major and well-funded organizations could possibly roll this back because it must be done in Washington."

The writer of these words of wisdom is not only a lawyer, but a farmer who farms. So, as all farmers, he understands the nature of gambling.

As to what I think? Since that first column, we now have in our little town access to the state lotto and scratch cards and keno, we have video gambling everywhere in South Dakota, which is 25 miles up the road. There are three Indian casinos and a gambling boat within 60 miles or so. Opportunities to lose money abound. (Notice I didn't say "win".)

The more gambling there is, the more worrisome it gets, at least to me. Paying for gas just last week in Phoenix, Arizona, I stood besides an unshaven young man with a little boy, both dressed in worn clothing. He was buying scratch card after scratch card, losing, losing, losing. Somehow, I had trouble justifying this because that money went for education or roads.

Understand, I don't mind a little foray into what some people think as dens of iniquity myself, betting my $20.00 worth of nickels. But I am aware of the scary pull to bet more and more, because the big win is surely coming. Is anybody immune to that?

The more gambling around, however, the less interested I've become. Too much of anything, eventually, makes a person sick. Familiarity breed contempt, they say, perhaps it also breeds wisdom.

Therein, lies our hope.

Some things to think about.

The Negative Spouse

The letter was short and to the point. I've altered it slightly to protect the innocent and the guilty, but it read, for the most part, as follows:

Dear Joanie; My spouse is so negative that it is depressing our whole household. Sure, times are tough this summer, but they aren't THAT tough. I need HELP!!!! It was signed: Hopefully, "Had it!"

Dear "Had it!" Much of what I write and speak about centers around the importance of thinking positively, and how that is a choice for each of us. Helping pessimists do that is not easy, but it's possible. We can't ever truly change another person, but we can help them change themselves. If not that, we can change ourselves. They will have to respond to that change.

Pessimists interpret events and think about people in negative terms. It's a habit. The internal conversation they have with themselves, which we call self-talk, always seems to dwell on the worst possible out come. If it doesn't rain, the crops will fail. If they make a mistake, the boss will fire them. If somebody tries to be nice, they must have an ulterior motive. They cannot rejoice in somebody else's good fortune.

They'd prefer you didn't either. Their job is keep everyone depressed.

Pessimists are bad medicine for others, but they are even worse for themselves. It's unhealthy to always think negatively, and it becomes a self-fulfilling prophesy. Just as being optimistic helps bring success. Studies show that people who go into surgery optimistically, for instance, are more likely to get well.

So what can we do? Well, first we need to tell them how their pessimism is affecting us. Not in a critical way, but in a caring, positive way. We can say, "I love you, and when you are so negative about everything it worries me, because it's not good for you. Besides, it hurts me and the whole family. It is imperative, for all of us, that you change. What can we do to help?"

It's a learning process. There are wonderful books that might help, Norman Vincent Peale being the first person to write about positive thinking, and still one of the best. If he (or she) shows a willingness to try, you might give him a signal when he starts being pessimistic, and help him view whatever it is in a more positive light.

There is another thing you can do, and this may sound really simplistic, but it works. Get him to take up a hobby, like golf, to take his mind off things he can't do anything about anyway, such as the weather. No matter how bad you feel, or how depressed you are, you can come off the golf course feeling worse BUT—you see the brilliance of this, don't you—it takes your mind off all your other troubles.

This comes to mind because recently I had the privilege of giving a little talk at the Scribner Grain & Lumber Company's 25 anniversary. Part of the celebration was a Monday afternoon golf tournament. At the end of the celebration Dennis Baumert, owner and manager, shook his head with a grin, and said, "Can you imagine, twenty-five years ago, getting 70 farmers out on the golf course on a Monday afternoon."

It's happening, all over the country. A plethora of farmers and their wives are golfing in our county, and I, for one, think it is wonderful for their mental and their physical health.

It's possible that your pessimistic mate will refuse to listen, or read, or change. If that happen, you must take care of yourself. *YOU* read positive books, get out with positive people, get a fun hobby and say many prayers.

Odds are that your positive attitude will rub off. Even if it doesn't, you have taken care of you. One way or another, I am POSITIVE you can make a difference.

Good luck!!

The Drug Fight Continued
(GOAD on HOLD)

Eight or nine years ago I read an article about drug dealers targeting grade school children, to "hook 'em young!" Thinking about Granddaughter Kate, I felt such rage I would have been capable of inflicting bodily harm on anyone who dared harm that child.

But what chance would I get to do that? I felt helpless. I thought, "Why doesn't somebody DO something?" And this annoying little voice that hangs out in my head, said, "So—why don't you?"

That was the day GOAD (Grandparents Outraged at the Abuse of Drugs) was born, with a membership of one. If other grandparents were as enraged as I was, we'd make a formidable team. I invited people to join via this very column, promising no dues and no meetings, just a sharing of important information. And they did!

My main goal, education, was accomplished by newsletters sent spasmodically. Education was necessary, I knew, because in earlier years illegal drugs ran rampant in our little town, and we—the parents—denied it, until it was almost too late for some of our kids. When forced to face it, we were shocked to learn drug dealers weren't "out there" somewhere, they were in our own back yard, adults selling to children, children selling to each other, kids we loved and respected and trusted, all part of this deadly game.

Thus motivated, I researched, wrote, edited, and ran the pages of my newsletter off on my copying machine, and coerced friends and relatives to help fold, envelope and stamp them. It was a job, especially when our membership grew past 500. Funding was no problem. Outside of a few kindly donations, it was my "cause." . Letters from members telling me how they had made a difference "armed" with our information, made it all worth while.

But soon great organizations of grant or government-funded professionals, such as Project Access of Norfolk, came into being. They teach, train, and send out informative newsletters that put mine to shame. And drug use was down. I pondered this.

So in our last Goad Newsletter, I asked members if they thought I should carry on. Only four responded. (My first clue.) One urged me to continue. Three said GOAD had served it's purpose gallantly, so put it to rest. The"rest" part sounded good to me. Feeling good, as if GOAD had served it's purpose, I put it to rest. Everything seemed to be in good hands.

And it is. Which is good because drug use is up again, abetted, studies show, by baby boomers who don't care much if their kids use drugs because they did, and they came out okay. Except for the ones who fried their brains. The war is on—again.

I've come to understand, however, that I don't have the clout to change things, no matter how passionately I'd like to. My only hope is that I can shine a little light on the problem areas to encourage and support the people who do have the clout.

For our children, that encouragement would come from educators, religious leaders, and parents, parents, parents. Grandparents can influence and cheer from the sidelines. But the parent is the deciding factor. The behavior they model, the expectations they have, the love they share, the time they spend, is what will make the difference.

Hang in there parents, one and all, we're cheering you on. Nobody ever said it was easy. But the rewards for your children and for you will last into eternity.

CHAPTER 7

Growing Old Gracefully

"Age is a Matter of Mind. If you don't mind, it doesn't matter."

(Mark Twain)

We Can Still Take Prisoners!!

It makes me feel good to know in the year of 1997 at 68 years of age, I am part of a national phenomena, the indisputable fact that people who are older now are much younger than people used to be when they are older. Nobody thinks I'm 68. Nobody I ask anyway. They all think I don't look a day over 67.

A couple of factors help us remain younger than our chroniclogical age might suggest. One is better health care, of course. More than that however, is *attitude.* A state of mind that refuses to succumb to the nattering of a few silly aches and pains, or the creaking of a bone or two. I am surrounded by 70, 80, and 90 year old friends who, concentrating on the positive, have knocked the smithereens out of the stereotypes about aging. I am grateful to them. I follow in their footsteps, kicking up my heels and howling at the moon, symbolically speaking.

I'm not talking about feeling young as in when we try to jump up after gardening and realize there's no way we're going to do that with even a modicum of dignity and grace.

I'm talking about feeling young because we get up in the morning knowing we have people we love who also love us, knowing we have things to do we like to do, flowers to raise and songs to sing, and realizing in the depth of our hearts and souls that we don't have to prove ourselves to anyone any more.

Been there. Done that.

I've included in this chapter several columns written through the years which express my militant anti-aging sentiments. In one, the column entitled "Empowerment" I share a poem written on this phenomena by a writer I greatly admire, Helen G. Moorhouse Crosswait. It's from "Coming Home." I share it so, thinking it over, you will understand, as I do, that we all can still take prisoners!

Empowerment

Go for it!!

A column has been germinating in my head these past months, but lacked just the right touch to come to fruition. Until, that is, a portion of a poem came my way. That did it.

I wrote the author, Helen G. Moorhouse Crosswait, for permission to use her wise words, and she sent them to me in her fine book, "Reflections of a Paleface From the Rosebud."

The column started incubating one evening as I was scrolling the TV channels for a likely program to serve as background to my perusal of the daily papers. I happened upon a fitness guru whose name, I am sorry to say, I do not remember. His teaching method consisted of much waving of arms, and wonderful silly putty facial expressions. That got my attention, but what interested me most as I settled in to listen, was his message. I knew, somehow, that it had a significance that would make a difference in my life.

What he said was that people always thought they needed to exercise more and more to get greater benefits. They would run more miles, for instance, but instead of the exercise being more effective, their bodies simply adjusted.

What they needed to do, he said, was not add time or distance to their run, but add spurts of intensity. Spurts of intensity rev up the body and do much good, in a cardiovascular sort of way.

The thought occurred to me that what's good for the body, spurts of intensity, would also be good for our minds and our souls.

As it happens, just this year, studies have come out indicating that keeping our minds active and challenged is greatly beneficial, and will help us avoid what happens when the mind deteriorates.

George Burns lived an active life until almost a hundred because he understood this concept. He said that the problem with some people is that they turn 65 and they think they have to act old. So they grunt when they sit down and groan when they get up, and pretty soon they've got the part. They're old.

Old or young, he said, people need to have something to do, somewhere to go, and something in their lives to be enthusiastic about. Consciously finding something to keep our lives "revved up" is a choice that we make for ourselves.

I've had the privilege to write about many people whom have made that choice, people who have suffered overwhelming adversities, but came through them not only surviving but thriving.

They've been an inspiration to me. They have a remarkable ability to celebrate what they have instead of dwelling on what they've lost. They make the most of things, living their lives with enthusiasm, with spurts of intensity, in spite of seemingly overwhelming difficulties.

It's not easy to get as excited about spurts of intensity when you begin to get —well—older. The body just gets to be something of a maintenance problem, and it's easier to just lay back in your recliner and groan. It is not allowed!!

Because—as a sage once wrote—*"You don't grow old by living a number of years, you grow old by giving up your ideals and losing your enthusiasm. Age wrinkles the skin, but if you give up enthusiasm, that wrinkles the soul."*

There's no excuse on God's green earth for a wrinkled soul. *Enthusiasm for life is something we can choose to develop by purposely adding spurts of intensity.*

If we challenge ourselves with something that tickles our fancy, if we rev ourselves up, as it were, we stay, literally and figuratively younger at heart.

Which brings me, at long last, to the wonderful poem that put this all in perspective for me, and I hope will for you, as we shuffle literally and figuratively through the glorious leaves of Fall.

Going Home

One goes along for what seems
millenniums—
calendar numbers fleeting
past your eyes—
years annihilating you physically
until by chance,
something happens,
and you must admit to some'
monumental effort
too relocate yourself, rejuvenate
and once again sense empowerment
and mentally you are still a lioness.
Suddenly you are grateful again
to be among the living
shuffling through glorious colored
leaves in Indian Summer.
You know you will yet take
some prisoners
because you are no longer
a prisoner of yourself.

Fighting the Arthritis War Together

(1993)

Kip says he's led an exciting life this year. He knows that every morning when he gets up he's going to have a pain, but he's not sure where it's going to be. The reason for his "exciting life" has been diagnosed as rheumatoid arthritis.

It has been my mission, ever since I realized what his problem was, to find a cure. I am willing for *him* to try anything, anything at all, to alleviate the pain. I've tried to talk him into everything from acupuncture, to mega doses of certain vitamins, to a radical diet, to a morning dose of raisins steeped in gin. (Joe Hish's remedy)

I get my ideas from friends, relatives and passing strangers. All of the above "cures" have worked for them, or so they say anyway. I've talked with strangers who cripple into elevators, or hobble down streets. I say "Arthritis, eh?" The reply is, "You better believe it!" And we discuss what they are doing that helps.

Many of our friends are also afflicted. Before Christmas I was talking to a friend who was concerned about Kip hobbling into church one Sunday. She said "How's he doing anyway?" I replied "The operation was a success, but he's having trouble with arthritis." She said "Tell me about it, I can hardly walk until noon."

And I get more "cures". I could give you example after example. Use heating pads. Take ice cold showers. Eat no fruit Eat no meat. Rest. Exercise. Go South. On and on.

Kip is pursuing a sensible medical course, experimenting with this and that, getting a little relief here, a little there, and last I heard, he was feeling much better. The reason I said "last I heard" was that this stuff is diabolical. One day a person can feel great, and move about with great agility. The next day that same person can be suffering from excruciating pain, and walking around as if he or she is 150 years old. As painful as it is to witness, those of us who don't have it can never really appreciate the frustration of those who do. Mostly, they don't talk about it, but you can tell by the way they move and the look in their eyes. I always know when Kip's feeling good, because he puts his boots on. When the arthritis is acting up in his feet, he wears his jogging shoes—even to cattle sales.

The problem is there are no real "cures." Specialists, such as Dr. William Palmer, the specialist who's working with Kip, say that the exact cause of rheumatoid arthritis is not known. It is thought to be brought on by an auto immune process. ("Auto-immune" meaning that your immune system, which usually protects you, turns against some of your own tissues.) In this disorder the synovium, a thin membrane surrounding a joint, gradually becomes inflamed and swollen, and this leads to inflammation of other parts of the affected joint.

And when it goes away—nobody is REALLY sure just why. Treatments that work with one patient won't work with another. In almost half the cases, according to statistics, patients recover completely. Other than that, people who are afflicted have to come to terms with what might be a permanent condition, pursue a course of treatment which gives them relief, and get on with life.

Not so easy to do. Not if you love golf and bowling. I've tried to convince Kip we can have fun with fishing, or photography, or things easier on arthritic joints. He doesn't buy it!

So along with half of America, including many of you who are reading this column, we battle on.

Good luck to us all!

Everyone Should Wear Purple (1993)

Years ago I read a piece by Jenny Joseph. I don't know who she is, but she made an impression on me. Purple started to creep into my wardrobe, along with bright colors of every hue. I found myself sloshing merrily through a mud puddle instead of carefully stepping on the dry spots. I picked wild flowers. I never did spit, but I contemplated it a couple of times.

The poem is a classic, and speaks words of wisdom to all.

"When I am an old woman,
I shall wear purple,
With a red hat which doesn't go, and doesn't suit me.
And I shall spend my pension on brandy and summer gloves and
Satin sandals, and say we've no money for butter.
I shall sit down on the pavement when I'm tired,
And gobble up samples in shops and press alarm bells
I shall go out in my slippers in the rain
And pick the flowers in other people's gardens
And learn to spit.
You can wear terrible shirts and grow more fat
And eat three pounds of sausages at a go
And only bread and a pickle for a week.
And hoard pens and pencil and beermats and things in boxes.
But now we must have fine clothes that keep us dry

> And pay our rent and not swear in the street,
> And set a good example for the children.
> We will have friends to dinner and read the papers.
> But maybe I ought to practice a little now?
> So people who know me are not too shocked and surprised
> when suddenly I am old and start to wear purple."

Now let's get one thing perfectly clear. I'm not sharing this from a "getting old" perspective. Not me. I am sharing this from the perspective that "life is too short to wait until we're old to wear purple." Purple, of course, is simply symbolic of the "don't take yourself so seriously" school of thought. It represents the "kick up your heels and having some fun" syndrome.

I'm getting better at this. This year I've dedicated myself to becoming really good at it. Nothing like a little hospital time with one's spouse to put one's life in perspective. Or one's self. I'm still ridden with "shoulds" and beset by deadlines, you understand, and I still have small guilt attacks when I'm not working on something productive. But I don't take all this as seriously as I once did.

I'm lightening up.

My dear and beloved Doctor Vlach, cautioning me to slow down after I had my warning blip on the dashboard of my life, (I fainted.) advised me as follows:

"Do the things you feel passionate about if you must, and the things that you really enjoy, but cut everything else out."

Although nobody believes me, I've been doing just that. I've turned down several requests to travel to far places because it would be more fun to be home. I've accepted some requests to go far places because it would be more fun than staying home. I've cut down on meetings, accepted only two speaking engagements a week, and marked off several weeks next year when Kip and I just plan to hang out together. Not bad for a confirmed guilt-ridden workaholic.

In the "really enjoy" category, I golf, bowl, play bridge, read books, spend time with loved ones, speak to groups just for the fun of it (including third graders and high school juniors), play the piano, write terrible poetry, and even cook..

I've decided on a New Year's resolution for all times of the year, and it will be "This year I will concentrate on enjoying what I enjoy." Every so often I look in the mirror and talk it over with my self. I'm presumptuous enough to think some of you may want to join me in this endeavor.

How often to we forget to enjoy what we enjoy?

I submit—too often! We are going so fast doing whatever it is we do that we forget to enjoy it. What a shame. What a pity!

Such things as hugging a friend who needs hugging, telling someone you love them, or stopping to smell the lilacs.

Lilacs are often purple you know.

Life Begins at Eighty

If you are eighty plus, I have good news for you!

The first 80 years are the hardest
The Second eighty are just a succession of birthday parties
Once you reach eighty, everyone wants to carry your baggage
and help you up the steps.
If you forget your address,
or anyone else's,
an appointment,
your own telephone number,
a promise to be three places at one time,
how many grandchildren you have,
you only have to say,
"I'm 80, you know."
Being seventy is no fun at all.
At that age they expect you to retire to a house in Florida
and complain about your arthritis. (They used to call it lumbago.)
When you reach 80,
Everyone is surprised that you are still alive.
They treat you with respect and are amazed
when you walk and talk sensibly.
So, try to make it to 80. It's the best time of life.
People forgive you for almost everything.
LIFE BEGINS AT 80!!

(AUTHOR UNKNOWN)

Getting Older With Enthusiasm

1995

An announcer on T.V. quoted Satchel Page as saying, "age is mind over matter, if you don't mind, it doesn't matter."

I was startled. Not by the statement, I believe it whole heartedly. I was startled by whom it was attributed too. I've always thought it was Mark Twain or Will Rogers, and lately, I've used it so much that I'd begun to think I thought it up myself.

The reason I've used it so much lately is that by the time you read this column I will have turned (gasp!) 67. I've looked over my birthday columns through the years, and the older I've gotten, the more militant I've gotten about staying young at heart.

You know, because I've told you enough times, that people don't grow old by living a whole bunch of years, they grow old by loosing their enthusiasm for life and giving up their ideals. Oh sure, our body just gets to be something of a maintenance problem after we slither past forty. We maybe have to write a few more notes to remind of us who we are and where we're supposed to be. Our skin might begin to really look like what it used to look in magnifying mirrors. But none of that is important if we maintain our enthusiasm for life. Age may wrinkle the skin, but if you give up enthusiasm it wrinkles the soul, and there's no excuse on God's green earth for a wrinkled soul. That happens in our heads.

When we've got a million hurts, psychologically and physically, how do we keep up your enthusiasm for life? I have some hints.

To my rescue comes my new friend Eddie, the 83 year old with the 21 year old Opal car, whom I introduced you to last week. She sent me a wonderful book called "A Touch of Wonder," by Arthur Gordon. His life enhancing essays include one in which he interviewed four older people who were dynamic, productive and alive, to asked them their secrets for staying so energized.

The first, a minister, said to stay renewed we had to *"give in to good-ness now and then."* Doing for others with no selfish end in mind leads to self-renewal.

The second, a philosopher, said *"Enthusiasm is the state of caring—really caring—about some thing."* We must look for enthusi-asm in others. *"When you find it those sparks will kindle flames in you!"*

The third, a psychiatrist said it's important to stop judging ourselves, to *"step out of our own shadow."* He said, *"The good in each of us far outweighs the bad, so be gentle with yourself, and let happiness and self-esteem and energy back into your life."*

The fourth was a widowed lady in his home town. Self-renewal, she said is *"just the old law of challenge and response....When you meet a challenge, something in you will respond."* So, don't be afraid to get involved, she said. When you see something that needs to be done, get in there and do it. You will come alive.

Gordon said to the widowed lady, *"I've talked to four older people and they've given me four different answers."* He told her what they were.

She said the answers were really not so different. They were all saying the same thing, something her grand mother always told her.

"Love life—and it will love you right back."

There you have it. Onward and upward!!!

Golf Not So Heavenly

(But would we want it to be?)

On a recent trip to Fairfield Bay, Arkansas, we met long time friends Jack and Terese Thielen of Denver, Col., and played golf. That's not as easy as it sounds.

Used to be we just slapped on a little sun screen and took off.

No longer. Jack and Kip, who both have aches and pains that get in the way of golfing their best, take pain pills first, and then begin to suit up.

Kip puts pepper patches on all the places that happen to be aching. He doesn't know if the pepper patches help, but they burn so much he forgets his other pain.

Jack has a bad back, so has to put on a girdle thingee for support, and then he puts a magnet in his pocket for a little added protection. Kip plasters Jack with pepper patches, and they throw on a few ace bandages, ankles, knees, etc.

Then we go out and have fun.

I'm just thankful we're out there. Not the "boys." They play very good golf on occasion, and when they don't, they complain. Constantly.

Even at worst, they get off some great shots and make a few spectacular putts, so you'd think that would be reward enough. Not so. Acceptance of lesser-than is hard for guys.

But—think about this—how much fun would it be to always be perfect?

Before our golf courses gets buried under the snow, and some of you fade into the southern climes, it would be good to meditate on a copyrighted poem by my good friend, avid-golfer, award winning writer, and the spirit of South Dakota, Bob Karolevitz. It first appeared in the Missouri Valley Observer. Bob wrote it after a friend said, "If they don't have golf in Heaven, I ain't goin'." It set him to musing..........

Heavenly Golf

They say there's golf in heaven, friends
    At least that's what I'm told.
The fairways are Elysian fields;
    The tees are purest gold

There are no trees, no traps of sand,
    No roughs to irritate.
You'll also find no water holes
    Inside the Pearly Gate.

The greens are billiard-table smooth
    So putting is a treat.
They also give you "gimmies"—
    Up to six or seven feet!

You'll find no stakes marked out-of-bounds,
    To complicate your score
I doubt if you have every seen
    A course like this before.

You get a bag of name-brand balls.
    (No x-outs in the lot.)
They come with miracles attached
    to guide each errant shot.

There's Mulligans on ev'ry hole
    For those who hook or slice,
And it is never counted if
    You whiff it once or twice.

You have your choice of caddies from
    Angelic Cherubim.
The problem is, with ev'ry stroke,
    They stop to sing a hymn.

Old golfing pros like Bobby Jones
    Are there to help your game.
If you don't shoot a sub-par round,
    You've no one else to blame.

The one thing that they always teach,
    Should come as no surprise.
If you would hit a mighty drive
    Don't lifteth up thine eyes.

They really frown on laggard play,
    I'm pleased as punch to tell.
When that occurs, St. Peter sends
    Slow foursomes straight to hell.

They are a few more drawbacks though,
    There is no Hole Nineteen.
You also have to watch your tongue
    And keep your language clean.

No beer, no gin, no whiskey highs,
    No gambling games allowed.
Your concentration's hampered by
    Those harps on every cloud.

It's also very boring when
    You birdie each Par Four
And aces are so common place,
    It isn't fun no more.

And so my friends, take my advice.
    It's this for what it's worth:
You'll find it more exciting if
    You play your golf on earth! (Amen!)

Today Is Cash In Hand

    Bumped into a man yesterday, who had an attitude of zestful living and appreciation of life. Kip and I, and cousin Barb Schultze of Omaha, were golfing on the Sun Land Village Golf Course here in Arizona, where we've holed up for a few weeks. A wiry little gentleman by the name of Bill joined us to make a foursome. That man could golf! He made me think in stature and ability of Barb's late husband, Bob. He hit the ball a country mile and putted with uncanny accuracy—with his wife's clubs. "I headed out in a hurry," he said, "and forgot to check and see who's clubs were on the cart." The longer we played, the more impressed I was with the man's golfing ability and his obvious enthusiasm for life.

No where near as impressed as I should have been, however. We were visiting on the 17 hole, waiting for the group ahead of us to get out of range, when we started to talk about things like patriotism and Veteran's Day. Bill said, just in passing, "I remember World War I, and I fought in World War II."

I gasped. "No way do you remember World War I," said I, having pegged him at about 70 years old, if that.

Anticipating my reaction, and enjoying it, he said, "I sure do. I was born in 1913."

The man was 83 years old! "Not only that," he added, "I feel great, and I don't take a single pill." That hardly seemed possible. Kip and I had to have a separate suit case just to get all our pills down here. It 's almost a given that when you get past fifty your body just gets to be something of a maintenance problem. Most of us have had things propped up, cut out, sewn together, replaced, or declared inactive. Not Bill!

While the state of his health might be unusual, his attitude is not. A multitude of people retire in Arizona. They are, for the most part, movers and shakers, and they remain that way, and they all feel great. They've certainly reached the age when most of them have aches and pains, but they don't whine about them. They wrestle them to the mat. They use everything from modern medicine to ancient medicine, from penicillin to herbs to acupuncture, throwing in exercise and yoga and line dancing just for kicks, and outside of a little squabbling about who's in charge of what, they have a fine time.

This is a generation of newly young elderly that are not about to sit down in their rocking chairs, wrap up in a shawl, and fossilize. I'm pleased and proud to be a part of this phenomena, having just turned (good grief!) 68, with more energy than I can remember having at 30.

I'm not kidding. I was tired when I was thirty. So I can attest personally to the indisputable fact that people who are older today are much younger than they used to be when they were older, or even when they were younger. We think younger. We act younger. And, by cracky, we ARE younger.

The factors that contribute to this phenomena are two. One is, of course, better health care and wiser eating habits. My mother used to butter her chocolate cake, for instance. And Dad Burney ate a piece of fat with every piece of meat that went in his mouth. Of course, Mom lived to be 85 and Dad 95, but most people who ate like that didn't live that long.

The biggest reason, however, is attitude. The attitude is best expressed by a bit of wisdom shared with me by a friendly stranger. "Yesterday is a canceled check. Tomorrow is a promissory note. Today is cash in hand." So, whatever age we are, it behooves us to spend it wisely and with enthusiasm.

CHAPTER 8

Encouraging Words
Poetry & Prose

On this journey we call life, we are often inspired, educated and amused along the way by the words of others. These words come to us just when we most need them, and not accidentally, or so I believe. Herein I will share some of the favorite bits of poetry and prose that have come my way. Some I share in the columns wherein I've used them as a focal point, and some I share much as they came to me, sent to me by readers, torn out of magazines, scribbled on place mats or church bulletins. They have gifted me with insights when I needed insights, and laughter when I needed laughter, and a couple of them even helped me release unshed tears. It is my fond hope—no—it is my expectation (!) that one or more of these is meant to be here just for you.

The Sun Will Always Rise—
Count On it!!

If ever we have proof positive of the mind-body connection, it's when the sun comes out. It's as if the clouds were lifted from our very souls. We feel better, the people around us are nicer. It's a different world.

On cloudy days, I have learned to bring the sun into my life by positive mental imagery. I envision my gardens. I love my gardens all year long, but I love them the most in January. Give me a seed catalog, and I'm transported into spring.

You know by now that I am a firm believer in this power we have in our minds. We CAN choose to bring sunshine into our own lives. My favorite line in the "Comes the Dawn" poem says it best, *"we can plant our own garden, and decorate our own soul, instead of waiting for somebody to bring us flowers." (See Keepers I & II)*

Furthermore, I believe that whatever task we're doing, whether it's typing on a computer, or cleaning the toilet, or giving a speech to 500 people, or sweeping a street, if we approach it positively, with a sense of mission, we do it with pride and satisfaction. Martin Luther King said, *"If it falls to your lot to be a street sweeper, sweep streets like Michelangelo carved marble. Sweep streets like Shakespeare wrote pictures. Sweep streets so well that all the hosts of heaven will have to say, 'Here lives a great sweeper who did his job well'."*

It's a fact that if things are going badly, you can mentally visualize them going better, and you start the process necessary to make that change. Whether it is in a relationship, on your job, in a sports event, or whatever.

I swear this is true, and I will give you an example. Take bowling. Please. You are probably sick of my bowling examples, but bear with me, it is my own little research area, and my colleagues can give you empirical evidence that what I say is true. My bowling has been very bad this fall. Atrocious. So bad that one week I bowled an 84. Split, split, split. I KNOW I can bowl better than that. So what was happening? Well, in the first place, I was not concentrating. Sports psychologists say that *athletes (?) do not lose their athletic ability, they lose their mental acuity, their concentration.* My mind was on a million other things. In the second place, when I bowled badly, I got discouraged, and before long I was expecting to bowl badly. My mind said, "Okay, if that's what you're thinking, that's what you'll do."

I had a little talk with myself, and realized that I'd not done any positive imaging all fall—about bowling. So the Monday night before we bowled, I visualized myself bowling well. I truly concentrated. I saw

myself getting strikes and picking up spares and than—to top it all off—
I visualized the score card that showed me with a 200 game.

I'd done that before. I could do it again.

Evidently, I convinced myself. I arrived at the bowling alley in
Crofton in a positive frame of mind. I just felt better. I believed. I bowled
two pretty good games, and then I bowled a 204. A 204 is not a terrific for
the good bowlers on our league, but for someone who's come off an 84,
it's a triumph!

Practice is important, and luck is always a factor, although for the
most part, we make our own luck. But believing we can is *most* important. Great coaches are successful because they've taught their kids to
believe in themselves.

I'm sure you get the message. It all has to do with the incontrovert-
ible fact that each of us has within us the ability to plant our own garden.

The Old Violin

We were visiting the other day about people who seemingly go down
for the count, but manage to survive and even thrive. Brought down,
often by forces which they didn't foresee, smothered in a landslide of bad
luck, they don't give up. They dust themselves off, pick themselves up,
and start all over again.

It's interesting to read the history of successful people. Their success
is often built on a string of failures. They learn from each failure, and
build on that knowledge.

In the agriculture business we have lots of resurrections of this sort.
There seems to be, in the depths of the souls of farmers and ranchers, the
determination and true grit of our pioneer forefathers who lived in the
most primitive conditions. They were beset by prairie fires and floods,
locusts, drought, rampant illness and marauding Indians, and somehow
still pulled through.

I'm convinced much of that tenacious ability to survive had to do
with the fact that our forefathers and mothers were people of great faith.

What brought this on is I was asked last week for a copy of a favorite
old poem which addresses this subject in such a way it stays with you
forever. It is called "The Old Violin." I found a copy for my friend—and,
of course, have decided to share it with all of you. Many of you have this
poem. Those of you who don't, need it.

The Old Violin

It was battered and scarred and the old auctioneer
thought it was scarcely worth his while
to spend much of time on this old violin, but he held it up with a
smile.
"Hey what am I bid, good folks:" cried he, "who'll start the bidding
for me.
A dollar once, a dollar now, and who'll go to three.
Three dollars once, three dollars twice, and going for three—but
no—
From the back of the room an old gray-haired man came forward,
and picked up the bow.
And wiping the dust from the old violin, and tightening up it's
strings,
He played—a melody so pure, so sweet—as sweet as the angel
sings.
And the music ceased, and the auctioneer, his voice now quiet and
low,
Said "What am I bid for this old violin," and then held it up with the
bow.
"A thousand dollar, and we'll go to two, two thousand and who'll go
to three.
Three thousand once, three thousand twice, and going and gone,"
said he!
And the people just cheered, except some of them cried,
"Now wait?" we just don't understand.
What changed it's worth" and the auctioneer replied,
"It was the touch of the Masters Hand."
And many of us get our life out of tune, and are battered and torn
within,
we'd be auctioned cheap to a thoughtless crowd, just like that old
violin.
A mess of potage, a glass of wine, a drink, and we travel on.
We're going once, we're going twice, we're going, we're almost
gone.
Except the Master comes, and the foolish crowd just never can
quite understand,
The worth of a soul, and the change that is wrought, by the touch of
the masters hand.

—David Lechart Smith

Building Your Town

Several years ago, a filling station owner, we'll call him "Mert," told me about a fellow who stopped by for gas. The man was dour and unpleasant, and had nothing good to say about anything or anybody. He told Mert he was driving around trying to find a "decent" place to live, and asked Mert, "What's your town like?"

Mert, a philosopher of sorts, asked. "What is it like in the town you live in now?"

"Terrible," the man said. "The people are unpleasant, nobody will volunteer for anything, I certainly wouldn't, the churches are full of cliques..." and on and on.

Mert thought this over for a minute, and then answered the dour man's first question, "I suspect you will find the same kind of town right here."

People pretty much find what they are looking for, don't you know.

People who do nothing but criticize are suspect. Have they tried to make a difference? Do they belong to the Chamber or any other fraternal organization? What committees do they serve on? Are they active in their church?

Or do they just gripe.

Mert's story came back to me this past week as I was visiting with a gathered throng in Columbus, Ne. I had the privilege of participating in the 1995 Columbus Days Prayer Breakfast, part of the renowned annual week-long celebration of "Columbus Days." The evening before, former Hartingtonite, Don Heimes, a past Columbus Chamber President and chairman of this event, and his wife, Pat, took me to their famed "Cheers"-like watering hole, the Husker House. Camaraderie was the order of the day. A wealth of interesting and colorful characters were interacting, so to speak, having a great time, and for a people-person like myself, it was a delight.

Amazingly, this same camaraderie was still present at seven o'clock the next morning. Special music by a quartet of Chamber members ("The Victory Voices") from the choir of St. Bonaventure church, set the tone. An enthusiastic crowd responded, and believe me, if you can gather an enthusiastic crowd at that hour, you have a Chamber of Commerce to be proud of.

For me, this has been a year of attending Chamber of Commerce celebrations, on one hand, and Prayer Breakfasts on the other. I like Prayer Breakfasts. They are a beacon of hope because they signify that important people think it is right to take time in the midst of this busy world to honor our spiritual connections.

I'm also pleased to work with Chambers, because is has become apparent to me as I travel to and fro, that a strong, dedicated Chamber of Commerce correlates directly with a "happening" community.

I belong to the P.R. wing of our Hartington Chamber, and my fellow members amaze me. They are enthusiastic participators. Want something done? Ask them. Some member will respond, without hesitation, "I can handle that."

Enthusiastic participation is the hallmark of a strong Chamber of Commerce. People invest their most precious and irreplaceable commodity, time, because it is well worth it. They build an esprit de corps with other enthusiastic participators, which is fun, and they have the deep satisfaction of knowing they have made a difference.

The only people who can do this for a town are the people who live there. The only people who can let a town mildew are the people who live there. If WE don't get involved in our cities, our churches, or our schools, wherever we live, we have no one else to blame for what DOESN'T happen.

I have a little poem, author unknown, that says this best. It goes like this:

If you want to live in a town,
That's the kind of a town you'd like,
You needn't pack your clothes in a grip,
And take a long, long hike.

Cause you'll find elsewhere what you left behind,
There's nothing that's really new.
It's a knock at yourself when you knock your town.
It isn't your town. It's you.

Real towns are not made by men afraid,
Lest somebody else gets ahead:
When everybody works, and nobody shirks,
You can raise a town from the dead.

And if you make it your personal stake,
Your neighbor will make it one too,
You town will be what YOU want it to be,
'cause it isn't your town, it's YOU.

Hug Them Now

(Anonymous)

If with pleasure you are viewing any work a person's doing,
If you like them, or you love them, tell them now.
Don't withhold your approbation till the parson makes oration,
And they lay with snowy lilies on their brow.
For no matter how you shout it, they don't really care about it,
They don't know how many teardrops you THEN shed.
If you think some praise is due them,
NOW'S the time to give it to them,
'Cause we sure can't read our tombstones when we're dead.

More than praise and more than money,
Is a comment kind and sunny,
And the hearty warm approval of a friend,
For it gives to life a savor, and it makes us stronger, braver,
And it gives us heart and spirit to the end.
So if they earn your praise, bestow it!
If you like them, let them KNOW it!
Let the words of true encouragement be said!!
'Cause we sure can't read our tombstones when we're dead.

Jump In and Scramble Through

I ran across a hand written note sent to me some time ago by a kindly reader, and it included a quote which she credited Richard Cardinal Cushing.

- "A great deal of talent it lost in the world for want of a little courage. Every day sends to their graves obscure ones whom timidity prevented from making a first effort; who if they could have been induced to begin, would in all probability have gone great lengths in the career of fame. The fact is, that to do anything in the world worth doing, we must not stand back shivering and thinking of the cold and danger, but jump in and scramble through as well as we can.

Give Me Your Smile, I'll Give You Mine

What is the nicest thing we can do this Christmas Season for our friends, our acquaintances, and passing strangers? Or any season at all, for that matter. What gift would cost us nothing, yet have untold benefits? Let me tell you. It's a smile. I don't mean a phony smile, although that is better than none, I mean a smile full of good will and acceptance, a smile with a hint of humor , and a smattering of love. Bear with me, I have proof positive.

We have no weapon more powerful on earth. Everybody smiles in the same language. A smile is so powerful that if we smile at ourselves in the mirror in the morning when we get up, phony smile or not, it sets a positive tone for our whole day.

I have seen a loving smile break down barriers of anger and frustration, soothe an aching heart, nourish a soul. Best yet, a sincere smile offends no one. It is a non-verbal, non touching, hug.

When I was young, and furious at my older sister June (which I was a lot) she'd put her hand on my forehead and hold me at arms length, me flaying away helplessly with my short arms, and she'd say, "You're going to smile!" over and over. I hated it. But I always smiled. And soon my outrage would dissipate into giggles.

It would be great if we could figure out a way to hold the world at arms length, speaking symbolically, until it came to it's senses about the futility of anger and hate. Then by some miracle the factions who claim to fight in the name of God would come to see that God is a God of love, not of war, and they could smile at one another.

Okay, so it's implausible. However, think about it, if ever we come close to accomplishing that miracle, it's at Christmas time.

If we can't make the whole world smile, we can do it for our own little corner of the world. Smiles are catching, you know. We can smile at loved ones, at harried sales clerks. We can share a compassionate smile with people who are hurting because of losses, for whom Christmas is especially painful, because we've all been there. As we sing in that beautiful hymn, Be Not Afraid, our smile says, "Blessed are those who weep and mourn for some day they shall laugh."

Unhostile laughter is the music of Christmas, the music of the soul, and smiles are the precursors of laughter, laughter is the beginning of faith.

Sometimes, at Christmas, we get confused about what is important. I do anyway. I love everything about Christmas, the carols, the lights, the parties and the presents. But I get can in a dither about these things, into a frenzy, if you must know, drowning out what I know only too well, which is that the most important thing about Christmas is not this hustle and bustle, this dispensing and accumulating of things. Christmas is about celebrating love, the love that emanates from the Child in the Manger, and suffuses the earth. If you read the latest Life magazine in which people of all beliefs discussed Jesus, even those who were not "believers" were amazed at how this kind and loving man continues to influence the whole world for good.

If all the extra curricular Christmas activities disappeared, and the celebration of love remained, that would be more than sufficient. Because the light of that love shines through us, and even those who do not hold with our Christian tradition are warmed by it.

The love is felt in the gathering of family and friends, in the warm memories that come in the door with every Christmas card. It's felt in the way we reach out to others.

I've been trying to figure out how to share these thoughts with you without being maudlin or overly sentimental or simplistic. It is essential for me to pause and meditate, and I thought you might like to join me. It helps us understand that the real celebration of Christmas is in our hearts, and when we accept that, we are suffused with the kind of peace that brings us down to earth while it lifts us up to heaven.

If that makes any sense.

It puts "celebrating" in it's proper perspective.

Not that I would give up the hoopla, not willingly, But if I had to choose, my sentiments were expressed in one of the first Christmas cards that came in our door. Expressing concern about too much bustle, and too many lights, too many parties, and too much food, and too many presents, it said,

> *Give me, instead, the fire's warmth*
> *Give me that great star of hope,*
> *Give me your smile*
> *And I'll give you mine.*

Happy Holidays, dear readers, where-ever you might be. God blessings on each and every one of you every day of the year.

Promoting Peace
People of All Faiths Working Harmoniously

I speak to the Lord in Catholic, but it is my firm belief, and I have the ecumenical credentials to show it, that we all speak to the same Lord, and that we have many more beliefs in common than the not so important things (in my mind) that separate us. I also believe we will not begin to make a dent in the problems in this sad old world until we, all God's children, start working together. If people of all faiths set the example by working harmoniously together, if we model the beliefs we claim to believe, those of little faith would have to sit up and take notice.

The problem, sometimes, is that our task seems overwhelming. Discouraging. We read the headlines, and see rampant materialism causing corruption in our politicians and even our religious leaders, and we think—what can we do?

Just everything, that's all. But we have to DO it. We can start by practicing forgiveness and love in our own families, our own churches, and our own communities, and we'll cause a ripple, like a rock in a pond, that will reach the distant shores. We may never know whom we've touched, but we need not. Sufficient to know every good that we do, no matter how small, makes a difference.

I ran across this prayer written by Archbishop Oscar Romera. It spoke to me, and I think will speak to you. I hope.

It helps, now and then, to step back and take a long view. The kingdom is not only beyond our efforts, it is even beyond our vision. We accomplish in our lifetime only a fraction of the magnificent enterprise that is God's work.
Nothing we do is complete, which is another way of saying the kingdom always lies beyond us.
No statement says all that could be said.
No prayer fully expresses our faith.
No confession brings perfection.
No pastoral visit brings wholeness.
No program accomplishes the church's mission.
No set of goals and objectives includes everything.
This is what we are about.
We plant the seeds that one day will grow.
We water the seeds already planted, knowing that they hold future promise.
We lay foundations that will need further development.
We provide yeast that produces effects far beyond our capabilities.

We cannot do everything, and there is a sense of liberation in realizing that.
This enables us to do something, and do it very well.
It may be incomplete, but is a beginning, a step along the way, an opportunity for the Lord's grace to enter and do the rest.
We may never see the end results, but that is the difference between the master builder and the worker.
We are workers, not master builders; ministers, not messiahs.
We are the prophets of a future not our own.

* * * * *

Something to think about!

Read the Handwriting on the Wall!!

Wandered over to Okibogee last weekend to gave a little talk for the Iowa Independent Banker's wives. I like talking to bankers because I was raised with them. Dad was a banker, Uncle Bert was a banker, brother Vince was a banker, cousin, Kenny Wales, is a banker, nephew Max is a banker, nephew V.E. is a banker, and even great nephew Scott (son of my niece Phyllis) is a banker. So, when I speak to Banker's wives, I feel as if I'm speaking to family.

Sometimes I am. Not a good idea. Last time I spoke to the Nebraska bankers my family and friends sat in the back row wearing black horned rim glasses and false noses. They looked better than usual, but it was a mite distracting.

I had been asked to give my humor speech and work in some of my Conquering Clutter workshop. I am the worst clutterer in the world, with the exception of my friend Gwen Lindberg of West Point. The reason I developed the workshop, which I start with,"I'm Joan, I am a clutterer," is because I know our pain. It's genetic, you know. My hand outs are full of tips that have even helped me.

I share this with you so you'll understand how I got to visiting with Neva Johnson from Algona, Iowa, a fellow clutterer. She had wise sayings to share. I loved them. They were so—well—wise.

The first one was "Busy clutter is healthier than idle tidiness." Fraught with wisdom, don't you agree? The second, equally fraught, was "Housework is the crab grass in the lawn of life."

Now on a roll, we started talking in axioms. Out of Neva's fertile mind came "If God had wanted me to touch my toes, he'd have put them on my knees." And when Kip came in to rush me out to get on with important things, like golfing, she wrote on my note pad, "I like life in the fast lane but I'm married to a speed bump."

In a banking and wise saying mode, I recalled the axioms my Dad had painted on the wall in the Bank of Hartington. Dad (E.W. Rossiter) survived the depression, lean and thrifty. So thrifty that he'd bring home a bar of candy on Sundays, cut it in pieces, and that would be our treat. And we were happy. Everybody lived frugally then. It affected me, however, because when I married Kip at 18 I was hoping for a whole bar of candy. In my dreams!

But that's another story. Dad was thrifty because he was sure the next depression was just around the corner. It was clear to him, but his customers didn't always see it, so he had painted on the bank wall: "Read the handwriting on the wall."

And, in case that was too subtle, he added: "This is the year to get in the clear!"

Those words burrowed into my sub-conscious, so when I married a cattle feeder, I was in for a shock. Kip lives by wise words too, passed down from generation to generation, the direct opposite of mine. They are:"You can't make money with your own money." The thinking was, with family stories to bear them out, one is too cautious with one's own money, and cattlemen—of all people—can't make money being cautious. So I've been told. And told! .

I'm curious, now, as I have been before, about the wise words that may be lurking in your mind. Words such as my Grandma Welches, "A stitch in time saves nine." (So?) Send them to me, will you, please? Or call, or tell me when I see you. I'll share, and it will be a good for all, because we will be, well—wiser—for them.

Wise Words

"It's not the things you do dear,
It's the things you leave undone,
That leave the bitter heartache
At the setting of the sun"

Thus spoke Eleanor Arens' Grandmother Richardson, to Eleanor, in this poem which, she writes,"pulled me out of the doldrums many a time." Also,'tis motivation to check our hearts before the sun sets.

Going to the mail box these past weeks has been fun, as wise sayings have been pouring in. Well, "enthusiastically trickling" anyway. We've gotten almost a hundred of them. I've been uplifted, inspired, and amused. The way things have been going around here lately, I needed all of that!

I will share some and save some. Some need to be pondered at length. Grandmother Richardson's would be one, it was so fraught with wisdom, but I couldn't wait to share it with you.

Mrs. Everett Waller from Holstein, Iowa, sent a bunch.A profound one, "Don't say it if you won't write it and sign it." leaves me wondering what we are going to at our card clubs. (Only kidding, girls!) Mrs. Waller, who also collects euphemisms, shared another axiom I fondly hope is true, "An ounce of mother is worth a pound of preachers."

Mary Pavlik of Norfolk, a teacher, shared one in she believes in whole heartedly, because she says "I have learned so much from my students." It is this: "Every adult needs a child to teach—it's the way *adults* learn!"

Guelda Jensen, a fellow writer from Stanton, developed a few axioms of her own to explain to herself and others why she was hooked on writing. They are, "It is a way to keep the cobwebs out of my brain," and "I have a little printer's ink in my blood." Most writers, me included, would attest to the truth of these wise words.

A page full of axioms came from my old friend, Anonymous. One I practice faithfully is: "Before you go to bed, give your troubles to God. He will be up all night anyway."

Here are a few more words to the wise.

*Blessed are those who can give without remembering and take without forgetting."

*Horse sense is seldom hitched to a waggin' tongue"

*Every person must live with the person he made of himself; and the better job he does in molding his character and improving his mind, the better company he will have.

*Teaching Kindergarten is like trying to keep 30 corks under water at the same time.

*Sign on Highway: "Driver who has one for the road, may have a State Trooper for a chaser."

My ulterior motive for soliciting these bits of wisdom to add to some I gathered years ago, is that I am working seriously (finally!) on my third book, and I've been looking for just the right quotes to head a couple of the sections. I found them!

In addition, however, I enjoy hearing from readers, even when I have to prod. No matter what the subject, readers letters always chase the cobwebs right out of my brain.

So, thanks for ALL your wise words, and God bless!

Favorite Adages that Bring a Smile

*There is so much good in the worst of us and so much bad in the best of us that it ill becomes any of us to find fault with the rest of us.

*A contented person is one who enjoys the scenery along the detours.

*A good friend is one who thinks you're a good egg even though you're slightly cracked.

*Life is like a piano—what you get out of it depends on how you play it.

*Help me not to worry, O lord, I feel like such a fool when everything turns out all right.

*Never let yesterday use up too much of today.

* Be what you is, because if you be what you ain't then you ain't what you be.

* Life is what happens when you're making other plans.

*A friend is one who knows you as you are, understands where you've been, accepts whom you've become and still—gently invites you to grow.

*Don't walk in front of me, I may not follow.
Don't walk behind me, I may not lead.
Just walk beside me and be my friend.

*To err is human, but to really foul things up requires a computer.

Success

To laugh often and much;
to win the respect of intelligent people and affection of children;
to earn appreciation of honest critics and endure the betrayal of false friends;

to appreciate beauty, to find the best in others;
to leave the world a bit better, whether by a healthy child, a garden
patch or a redeemed social condition.
to know even one life has breathed easier because you have lived.
This is to have succeeded.
—Ralph Waldo Emerson

Thinking!

If you think you are beaten, you are.
If you think you dare not, you don't.
If you'd like to win, but you think you can't,
It's almost a cinch that you won't.
If you think you'll lose, you've lost.
For all over the world we find,
Success begins with a person's mind.
If you think you're outclassed, you are.
You've got to think high to rise.
You've got to be sure of yourself
Before you can win a prize.
Life's battles don't always go,
To the stronger or faster man.
But sooner or later, the man who wins,
Is the man who thinks he can.

The Teacher Was Right;
Now I Understand

The following poem was read by Father Tony Tresnak at the funeral of
a dear young friend whose brilliant career was ruined and, ultimately, his
life lost because of his unsuccessful battle with alcohol. Father Tony, who
understood that "terrible burden" as only a recovering alcoholic can,
brought to that funeral Mass a great piece of himself. Knowing how hard it
is to understand these things, or anything much at all in this sad old world,
he shared the following prayer. It was a comfort. Father Tony died in the
spring of 1997, after a prolonged and painful illness. My sister Anne and I
visited him a short time before he died, and marveled at his wit and wisom

in the face of all he was enduring. His only comment was, "I have had better days." Sitting at his funeral Mass at the Great Cathedral in Omaha, filled with the multitude of priests, relatives, friends and the young people who loved him, I remembered his poem. And singing the final hymn, the one he'd requested in his will, "Morning has Broken" I knew that he now "understood" and "better days" were his. And I also knew, most assuredly, that his gentle spirit and his love would remain with us.

Hope this will be a comfort for you, too.

"The Folded Page"

Up in a quaint old attic,
As raindrops patter down,
I sat paging through an old schoolbook—
Dusty, tattered, and brown.

I came to a page that was folded down.
And across it was written in childish hand:
"the teacher says to leave this for now,
'tis hard to understand.

I unfolded the page and again read,
Just as the teacher planned,
Then I nodded my head and to myself said,
The teacher's right, now I understand.

Many pages in the book of life,
do not read as planned,
All we can do is fold them and write:
The Teacher says to leave this for now, 'tis hard to understand."

Then—perhaps in Heaven—there'll come day,
we will unfold the pages and,
read them again and say,
The teacher was right; *now* I understand.

Father Tony went on to say.
When it comes to the death of the person whom we're laying at rest today, about all we can do is fold the page down and write "The Teacher says to leave this for now, 'tis hard to understand."

He included in his homily the following poem.

"All which I took from thee
I did but take not for thy harms,
But just that thou might seek thy rest,
In the warm comfort of my arms."

Prayer for Bad Times

Dear God: Help me to be a good sport in this game of life. I don't ask for an easy place in the lineup. Put me anywhere you need me. I only ask that I can give you 100 percent of everything I have. If all the hard drives seem to come my way, I thank you for the compliment. Help me remember that you never send a player more trouble than he can handle.

And, help me, Lord, to accept the bad breaks as part of the game. May I always play on the square, no matter what the others do. Help me study the Book so I'll know the rules.

Finally, God, if the natural turn of events goes against me and I'm benched for sickness or old age, help me accept that as part of the game, too. Keep me from whimpering that I was framed or that I got a raw deal. And when I finish the final innings, I ask for no laurels. All I want is to believe in my heart that I played as well as I could and that I didn't let you down. (Richard Cardinal Cushing.)

To Those I Love

If I should ever leave you
whom I love
To go along the Silent Way,
grieve not,
Nor speak of me with tears,
but laugh and talk
Of me as if I were
besides you there.
(I'd come—I'd come,
could I but find a way!
But would not tears and grief
be barriers?)
And when you hear a song
or see a bird

I loved, please do not let
the thought of me
Be sad...For I am
loving you as
I always have...
You were so good to me!
There are so many things
I wanted still
To do—so many things
to say to you...
Remember that I
did not fear...It was
Just leaving you
that was so hard to face...
We cannot see Beyond...
But this I know:
I loved you so—'twas heaven
here with you!
(Clark Clifford wrote this poem for an old friend)

What God Has Promised

God hath not promised
Skies always blue,
Flower-strewn pathways
All our life through;
God hath not promised
Sun without rain,
Joy without sorrow,
Peace without pain.

But God Hath Promised
Strength for the day,
Rest for the labor,
Light for the way,
Grace for trials,
Help from above,
Unfailing sympathy,
Undying love.

—Annie Johnson Flint

Twilight Prayer

May He protect us all the day long,
    'till the shades lengthen
    and the evening falls and the busy world is hushed
    and the fever of life is over
    and our work is done.
Then in His mercy,
    may he give us safe lodging
    and holy rest
    and peace at the last. Amen

(Cardinal Newman)

Only YOU Know My Type, Lord

On Sunday, April 14 of the year, 1996, I journeyed to Omaha to give a little talk at the behest of Randy Grosse, then President of St. James Parish Council. Randy is also a writer, and he presented me with a beautiful framed copy of a poem which seemed to speak just to me. It sits on my desk now, and is my favorite prayer.

The poem took on a new perspective the Sunday of the gospel on loaves and fishes, because of a homily given by our Deacon Paul Albenesius. Deacon Paul started his sermon with a lovely story about growing up at home where his mother, Christine, served fried chicken every Sunday. His description of his mom browning the chicken to put in the oven to bake was so vivid I could hear the sizzle and smell the chicken.

Almost every Sunday, Deacon Paul said, unexpected company dropped in just in time for dinner, so their Sunday meal had to be stretched to accommodate them. Sometimes younger members of the family, of which Deacon Paul was one, were left with hot dogs.

No one, not even Deacon Paul, would pretend giving up chicken for a hot dog was fun. But what he did with that example was bring the meaning of Sunday's gospel home. Been there. Done that.

He then segued nicely into our need to share not only food, but ourselves. A perfect example being the folks who take communion to shut ins. He pointed out that any good deeds we do for others, as volunteers, or on our jobs, or in our family, is the work of the Lord. If we look around, he said, we might see a few places where we could do even more, mentioning a few that hit home with me.

I firmly believe, if we offer up our day, anything we do is a prayer. Golf, even. Not for me, of course, but for avid golfers who give it their all. The athlete's at the Olympics praised the Lord magnificently, many of them praying, some making the sign of the cross. Point is, we can emulate the Lord's generosity in many ways.

Which brings me back to our giant sized Deacon, Paul Albenesuis. He could have been a discus thrower, or a weight lifter, or a basketball player, and praised the Lord this way. He choose, instead, to be a priest, the ultimate gift to the Lord, and to us all.

That's when I realized that my (?) poem, while it gives me the special jolt I need to stay the path, really speaks to every one. So I decided to share it with you. I hope you like it as much as I do.

Only you know
my type
Lord,
So I'm glad
You're the typesetter.

Reset my life
I pray
in bold script,
personal, beautiful
like Jesus.

Make me a page clean,
fresh, well inked
on which all may read
the proofs
of Your existence.

(by Elise Hatfield)

I'd Pick More Daisies

If I had my life to live over, I'd try to make more mistakes next time. I would relax. I would limber up. I know few things I would take seriously. I would be crazier. I would be less hygenic. I would take more chances. I would climb more mountains, swim more rivers and watch more sunsets. I would burn more gasoline. I would eat more ice crean and less beans. I would have more actual troubles and fewer imaginary ones. You see, I am one of the people who live prophylactically and sensibly and sanely, hour after hour, day after day.

Oh, I have my mad moments, and if I had it to do again, I'd have more of them. In fact, I'd try to have nothing else. Just moments, one after another, instead of living so many years ahead. I have been one of those people who never go anywhere without a thermometer, a hot water bottle, a gargle, a raincoat and a parachute. If I had it to do over again, I would go more places and travel lighter than I have. If I had my life to live over again, I would start barefooted earlier in the spring and stay that way later in the fall. I would play hockey more. I would ride on more merry-go-rounds. I'd pick more daisy's.

—Betty Holbrook

****

I'd smell more lilacs.
I'd buy more hyacinths for my soul.

—Joan Burney

Epilogue

A year ago friends of ours had a shower for to-be-born Abbie, daughter of Chuck and Kathy. It was on the Sunday of Hartington Hog Holidays, so, before the shower, Kathy's mom, Carol Cranston, and I, visited the "Pigcasso Craft Show" and the "Pigs in a Blanket" quilt show. Carol, a superb quilter, commented on the excellence of the quilts. I, a no-talent nerd when it comes to fancy sewing, just looked with awe. The quilts that really caught my eye, however, were those made especially for Fiftieth Anniversaries. Each child and grandchild of the celebrating couple had sewn one of the squares in the quilt. The end result was a spectacular display of artistic ability and love, and, since families tend to be large in our county, a very large quilt.

Later, at the shower, I got to laughing about how impossible it would be for Kip and me to have such a quilt on our Fiftieth Anniversary. With six kids and three grandchildren, it would have to be a lap robe, or have giant blocks. And, considering their ability with fancy work and wacky senses of humor, I could only imagine what those blocks would be. Envisioning this we all laughed heartily, and I forgot about it.

However, to my daughter Juli, I'd just thrown down the gauntlet.

That's why, when we walked into the Hartington Country Club for the Open House the kids hosted, and I saw what was hanging on the wall, I dissolved into tears. There was a quilt–a huge one. Painstakingly, the four conspirators, Juli, John, Lou Ann and Kate, transferred the pictures of Kip and I, from baby-hood to our present antiquity, to cloth, and then sewed them into a patchwork quilt that told the history of our lives. Each handled their own area of expertise (Juli sneaking pictures from home, John running the technical part, Lou Ann and Kate handling most of the quilting, all contributing artistically) and produced, on the behalf of all our brood, a quilt to end all quilts. A unique one of a kind heirloom. Where we will display it, I do not know, but display it we will. Nothing in this whole world would have pleased me more.

With that emotional start, we experienced a day that will also be a one of a kind heirloom in our hearts. Truly, our lives walked through those doors. Folks we have laughed with and cried with and loved; relatives and friends from afar, from next door, and all places in between, each one an irreplaceable square in the crazy quilt of our lives. Those who could not be there for whatever reason let us know, in various ways, that they were with us in spirit. We stored up enough hugs to last forever.

I'm writing this column with the sense that I am echoing the sentiments of the many couples celebrating fiftieth anniversaries this year. You've doubtless seen our pictures. 1947 was the year after the war ended.

Our men came home in a marrying mood. We're wondering if a year like this will ever happen again, given the divorce statistics. We know for many reasons, but especially when we hug friends who are widows and widowers, that we are darned lucky.

The kids' party was like them. Spontaneous, informal and fun. We tried to make a brief truce with the problems that beset us and those we love, and simply enjoy the moment, celebrating the fact that we'd all survived with some degree of enthusiasm.

Simply saying thank you for the patience, love and support of our own family, friends, and the many readers who've become a part of our lives doesn't seem adequate for the well of emotions that flood me as I write this column. But it's all I have. So, thanks to all of you who have made the patchwork quilt of our lives so colorful and so beautiful. God bless you all!

An Ancient Blessing

May the blessed sunlight
shine on you and warm your heart
until it glows like a great fire,
so that a stranger may come and
warm himself at it. May God
always bless you,
love you and keep you.